CW01373745

# FREEDOM FOR PUBLISHING
# PUBLISHING FOR FREEDOM

# FREEDOM FOR PUBLISHING PUBLISHING FOR FREEDOM

## *The Central and East European Publishing Project*

EDITED BY

Timothy Garton Ash

WITH CONTRIBUTIONS FROM

Ralf Dahrendorf
Richard Davy
Elizabeth Winter

CENTRAL EUROPEAN UNIVERSITY PRESS
Budapest London New York

First published in 1995 by
Central European University Press
1051 Budapest
Nádor utca 9

Distributed by
Oxford University Press, Walton Street, Oxford OX2 6DP
Oxford New York Athens Auckland Bangkok Bombay Toronto
Calcutta Cape Town Dar es Salaam Delhi Florence Hong Kong
Istanbul Karachi Kuala Lumpur Madras Madrid Melbourne
Mexico City Nairobi Paris Singapore Taipei Tokyo Toronto
and associated companies in Berlin Ibadan
Distributed in the United States
by Oxford University Press Inc., New York



British Library Cataloguing in Publication Data
A CIP catalogue record for this book is available from
the British Library

ISBN 1–85866–055–6 Paperback

Library of Congress Cataloging in Publication Data
A CIP catalog record for this book is available from the
Library of Congress

Designed, typeset and produced by John Saunders
Printed and bound in Great Britain by
Biddles of Guildford, Surrey

# *Contents*

# *Editorial Note*

In our work in the Central and East European Publishing Project we made great efforts to give everyone, and every book and periodical, the dignity of his, her or its proper name – including all accents and diacritical marks. Given the staggering variety of accents and diacritical marks that would be involved in this book, and for reasons of speed, simplicity and economy, we have reluctantly decided to dispense with all but the most common accents.

We would like to thank Sally Laird, Laurens van Krevelen, Peter Kaufman, Euan Henderson, Lynette Owen, Vera Ebels, Gyorgy Bence, David Foster, Jerzy Jedlicki and Danuta Garton Ash for their comments on all or part of the typescript, and Barbara Bunyan and Marilyn Cox for their expert preparation of it.

The cover incorporates a logo designed for the Project by Jiri Kolar. We are most grateful to Mr Kolar for permission to use it here.

*Oxford, March 1995* T.G.A.

# *Introduction*

RALF DAHRENDORF

This book tells a success story. It is the story of a small private foundation making its own contribution to encouraging the new liberty of Central and Eastern Europe. The foundation was called the Central and East European Publishing Project: CEEPP. Attempts to give it a more enticing name failed, as Timothy Garton Ash, the inventor of the Project, describes in his account of its history in this book. Perhaps this is as it should be. The Project was just that – a project.

It began when the Berlin Wall still seemed a solid structure for decades to come; it helped in weakening its stability; it assisted in the often painful process of transition. In the end, CEEPP put an end to its activity of its own accord. The reason is most certainly not that "the return to normality" is yet complete: more will have to be done, and it will be done by future generations. The reason is rather that a small organisation based more on the enthusiasm of its members than on funds has its useful life-cycle, especially if it had the good fortune to accompany the dramatic changes in Europe before and after 1989. Unusually but deliberately, it was decided to close down the Oxford Project at the end of 1994.

This book tells the story in four parts. First of all, Timothy Garton Ash describes the Project's history in his own inimitable style. He thought of it; he was instrumental in persuading foundations to support CEEPP; he gave it many a push throughout its life and sometimes carried our support to its addressees in his own suitcase. All this and more can be found in his story.

Secondly, we thought it useful to provide a catalogue of activity, an annotated catalogue to be sure. A "catalogue of activity" in the case of a project concerned with publishing is, to a large extent, a bibliography, a list of books and journals which might not have appeared if we had not identified them as worthy of some support. This catalogue was produced by our Project Director, Elizabeth Winter. With Sally Laird, Project Director 1990–1992, Danuta Garton Ash, our Consultant since 1992, and our successive Assistant Directors, Alison Oldfield and Maria Williamson, she represented the office of the Project. For the post-1989 period this office was physically located in the immediate vicinity of St Antony's College, which helped the Project intellectually as well as practically. It is worth mentioning that most members of the Project office worked on a part-time basis.

The third part of the book is an eminently readable and at the same time informative account of the state of publishing in the "Visegrad" countries, with which we were above all concerned, concluding with suggestions for further Western help. Richard Davy, who produced this account for CEEPP, added specific information to his already profound knowledge of the region.

Finally, we have added a "dessert" which may give readers an idea of the fun we had despite the seriousness of our task: a list of one hundred books which – in the view of those who composed it – had a major influence on Western public discourse since the Second World War. We were inspired to produce such a list by frequent requests from Central and East European publishers for titles which should be translated, although we are not suggesting that our list of one hundred books is necessarily a publisher's list for the new democracies.

What was CEEPP about? One phrase which we used frequently was that it made a contribution towards creating "a common market of the mind" in Europe. Not everyone likes the word "market" in connection with matters of the mind, though authors, editors, and above all publishers in the post-communist world have now learned that they too cannot escape the constraints of the market. But we meant something else. We meant the marketplace in the old liberal sense, the place where ideas are exchanged, and where by their exchange they generate new ideas, the "public" in the best sense of that word. We wanted it to become one public again, one marketplace of discourse.

The process is difficult and still far from complete. Neither East nor

West can simply absorb the history of the other. The German example shows how deep different historical experiences go; East and West Germans still read different newspapers and to some extent even different books, though the book market is becoming more united. Our list of one hundred books gives some indication of what fortunate Westerners found important in the last fifty years. CEEPP has also supported translations the other way, from East to West, though not of course of the barren "literature" of socialist realism. Perhaps we – the Europeans of East and West – need common experiences before we can fully appreciate the different memories which we bring to bear on them. Thus the common market of the mind needs more efforts like ours, and above all, more time.

There is one other concept which describes what CEEPP was about, civil society. Since this concerns the Project itself as well as its objectives, it may be worth a few moments of reflection. Civil society describes that part of our lives which is not determined by governments. In an illiberal world, civil society is built in opposition to the state; the memory lingers in the post-communist countries as it did, and still does, in post-fascist countries. In an open world, civil society is simply the ordinary medium of life, the untidy universe of organisations and institutions, of small businesses and universities and local communities and associations of many kinds in which we spend our days. It is neither for or against the state, but independent of it. Civil society is truly autonomous. It does not borrow its birthright from governments or other authorities.

Publishing is a central part of civil society. Newspapers and journals and books are perhaps the most visible index of whether there is an autonomous sphere of associations or whether government determines all. Today we know that such autonomy is at risk not only from governments but also from private monopolists. Half a dozen names account for a very large portion of European publishing, East and West, and raise new questions of liberty. Civil society cannot survive in a world of cartels and monopolies. A new battle may well have to be fought in this regard. It is, however, important precisely because publishing is at the heart of civil society.

One other aspect of civil society worth mentioning in this context is foundations. CEEPP was a foundation, under English law a trust. This again means that it was not in any sense a governmental organisation. We were fortunate in finding funders both in the United States and in Europe who were prepared to entrust us with their funds. The disbursement of the funds was left in the hands of the trustees, initially a small group of seven, later eleven individuals. These were trustees not as representatives of countries or foundations or any other extraneous body, but as informed and enthusiastic supporters of the cause. Of course, CEEPP had to report to its funders on what it had done, and naturally questions were asked about the general direction as well as about specific grants. But basically the trustees operated as an independent group, not for any personal gain but for a public purpose.

I have long regarded foundations as one of the keys to the reality of civil societies. They are, to be sure, not equally strong in the different parts of the free world. Originally probably an English idea, foundations have become one of the wonders of American society. In the United States, the central state is still relatively weak. Many social issues can only be dealt with by private initiative. Foundations have become the vehicle of such philanthropy, with the great names of American economic history reappearing in different guises: Ford, Rockefeller, more recently MacArthur, and in our area of activity, Soros. All of these have supported CEEPP to a greater or lesser extent.

In Europe, foundations have found the environment less friendly. Britain has a great philanthropic tradition, but today per capita support for charities amounts to no more than one-tenth of that in the United States. Continental Europe takes us to a different dimension again; its philanthropic sector amounts to one-tenth of that of Britain. In other words, for every dollar given to charity on the European Continent, ten are given in Britain, and a hundred in the United States. This reflects the varying role of the state in different parts, and with it the varying strength of civil society. Must we assume that by the same token it also reflects variations in the stability of the open society?

Foundations are delicate and complicated institutions. Even in the United States it has taken a long time for them to become as confident and solid as they are today. The main point is that while their sponsors are obviously crucial for their existence, the idiosyncrasies of sponsors must not determine the work of foundations themselves. Put more crudely, the talent which it takes to make money is very different from the talent which it takes to spend money sensibly for philanthropic purposes. I remember the time – I was then a Trustee of the Ford Foundation – when Henry Ford III objected to our spending so much on the poor and the disadvantaged because he thought that helping the poor is by definition a left-wing cause.

Since then, the Ford Foundation has changed a great deal. As one of the main sponsors of CEEPP it has acted in an exemplary fashion towards us, and I hope that we have repaid its hands-off attitude by responsible decisions.

One particular observation about Europe needs to be made; it is relevant both for foundations and for publishing. When one sets up a small trust like the CEEPP, one needs a certain amount to keep the office going. This should be a modest amount. In my view no more than 15 per cent of total expenditure should go on administration, though such figures are in one sense dubious because the administration of small organisations is often indistinguishable from their substantive activities. However, a certain amount of core funding is needed. One might even say that the civil society needs some core funding. European benefactors find it hard to accept this fact. As a result, many European organisations turn to their governments, or nowadays to the European Union, for their core funding and thereby betray their civil society purposes. If they do not turn to government, they turn to American foundations, to "Ford" which has such a splendid record in this respect. One must wish that Europeans will learn from Americans as regards core funding because it is surely unlikely that American foundations will continue to finance European ventures at a time at which Europeans themselves should have the ability and the money to do so.

There is one other point where Europeans would do well to follow the best American examples. For the most part, European foundations are reluctant to spend their income outside the national boundaries in which they were created. Some have specific programmes relating their country with another one, e.g. Germany and Poland. But the European Cultural Foundation in the Netherlands is still unusual in its Europe-wide scope, and we were fortunate to benefit from the outset from its internationalism.

Thus CEEPP has made a contribution to civil society in two respects. It has promoted publishing, and it has done so as a foundation. The Project has also done one other thing, which is to assist the setting up of associations which can carry on the work initially supported from Western sources. Publishers' associations are only one example. The CEEPP internship programme may well have helped not only publishers but also their organisations. But this was only a part of our intentions. Civil society is not an organised "corporatist" cartel of associations; it is a lively, at times, chaotic multiplicity of activities. The Journals' Workshop which we organised gave a wonderful example, and while most journal editors asked for, and will continue to ask for, subsidies, their variety and diversity are themselves elements of civil society.

It is nice to tell a success story. Yet there is obviously no reason for euphoria. The "return to normality" itself means that a whole lot of problems arise which may be familiar to us in the old West but which appear anything but normal to people in the new democracies. We know that journals are born, live, and die, sometimes before they have lived for any length of time. We know that books, even good books, do not necessarily sell. The fact that those who at last have joined the free world are making such discoveries now, is no reason for satisfaction. It is hard to be an author, and painful to try and reconcile one's aspirations with the vagaries of "the market". It is even harder to be the editor of a journal, especially in countries in which other media, such as the Saturday or Sunday editions of newspapers, compete. It may not be quite so hard to be a publisher, though the dilemma of cultural intent and market success raises many questions for us, the concerned citizens. But all these are matters which we now share all over Europe. To this extent, at least, the common market of the mind has come about.

When I was asked to serve as Chairman of CEEPP, my commitment to liberty was much greater than my knowledge of either East and Central Europe or of publishing. This is still true, though I have learned a great deal in the nine years over which the Project has lasted. My *Reflections on the Revolution in Europe* would probably not have been written without the early CEEPP experience. At that time, there were seven of us: Timothy Garton Ash, of course; the brilliant French sceptic who always remains committed to freedom, François Furet; the very European American whose heart is such a good judge of minds, Jane Kramer; the ever thoughtful Dutch publisher, Laurens van Krevelen, who does not show his emotions but acts on them; the deeply convinced European, Raymond Georis, who never tires of seeking an effective wider Europe; the warm-hearted, courageous, almost classical Swedish intellectual, Per Wästberg. Later, after 1989, three Central Europeans joined the original seven: Eda Kriseova, the Czech writer whose charm lies in the unity of her heart and her mind, her sincerity as a person of independence; Jerzy Jedlicki, the Polish historian who weighs his judgments carefully but never wavers in his liberal creed; and Gyorgy Bence, the Hungarian philosopher, a true internationalist whose irony cannot conceal the beliefs which he shares with others who have had to fight for their freedom.

It may seem an irrelevance to say so, but the CEEPP was, despite its bureaucratic-sounding acronym, fun. Those involved enjoyed what they were doing while obviously taking it seriously. I hope that this book conveys a little of the enjoyment as well as the excitement of our enterprise. Beyond that, it remains for the departing trustees of a small but significant venture in liberty to wish all the best to their successors, led by Laurens van Krevelen as head of the Dutch Fund for Central and East European Book Projects. They have an important job to do. Perhaps this memoir can encourage them to embark on the next stage of the journey to freedom, and their supporters to give them the sustenance for the trip.

# *The History of CEEPP*

TIMOTHY GARTON ASH

The nine years of the Central and East European Publishing Project straddle the largest watershed in European history since 1945, possibly even since 1917. Because of the nature of the Project's work, its history also illuminates the nature of the changes in Central and Eastern Europe across the watershed of 1989.

When the original group of seven founder members first met, in Brussels in March 1986, the division of Europe which we knew in shorthand as "Yalta" was still very much in place. Gorbachev had come to power exactly one year before, but the thaw in what we then habitually called "East–West relations" was only just getting under way. In Honecker's East Germany, in Husak's "normalised" Czechoslovakia, in Jaruzelski's Poland, there were still political prisoners, censorship, and repressive post totalitarian regimes. Travelling to Warsaw or Prague, let alone crossing the Berlin Wall, you passed through what was still recognisably the iron curtain.

When we gathered for our final meeting, in Oxford in December 1994, it was a very different Europe, and a Central Europe transformed out of all recognition. Not just the Berlin Wall but the very state of East Germany had ceased to exist. Czechoslovakia had become free but then split in two. For Poland the question was no longer whether but rather when it would join NATO and the European Union, as the EC had, in the meantime, become. Several of those we first knew as samizdat publishers, translators or exiled writers were now ambassadors, ministers or even presidents. The whole world of book and journal publishing with which we primarily dealt was changed utterly. As a small symptom of these changes, a Czech writer, a Polish historian and a Hungarian philosopher, all three with personal experience of opposition and political persecution behind them, now sat among us as trustees.

So this is not just the short official history of a small organisation. It is also a small contribution – a footnote, if you will – to the history of that great transformation. It falls naturally into two parts: before and after.

## BEFORE (1986–1989)

The origins of the Project can be described in two different ways. On the one hand, and quite practically, a number of foundations wished to do more to support Central and East European publishing, and translations from those languages. It was this consortium of foundations (see list on page 48), led by the Ford Foundation and the European Cultural Foundation, who asked Ralf Dahrendorf to chair what they described as "an international committee of leading authorities on European culture and public affairs as well as persons experienced in book and magazine publishing" to guide the Project.

As soon as it met, however, the international committee took on a life of its own, and the second way of describing the origins of the project would be to look at the motives and interests of the founding members (see list on page 48). Per Wästberg, for example, who was then President of International PEN, recalls that his interest in this whole area was stimulated by participating in an unofficial symposium organised by the International Helsinki Federation for Human Rights in Budapest, to coincide with the official CSCE meeting on cultural cooperation. (I have described this interesting event in my *The Uses of Adversity*.) François Furet, the historian of the French revolution, was inspired by the intellectual debate on "Central Europe" then being conducted in Paris under the influence of Milan Kundera. And so one could go on, round the table.

At this first meeting in Brussels a number of basic decisions were taken. We agreed that the overall objective was to be that of promoting "a free flow of culture between East and West Europe". Our assumption was that the geopolitical division of Europe – the iron curtain – had interrupted the normal and healthy flow not just of people but also of books and ideas. Ralf Dahrendorf coined the phrase "a common market of the mind". "It was agreed," the minutes note, "that the programme was not intentionally political, let alone propagandist." Yet we were surely well aware – at least speaking for myself, I was certainly very well aware – of the political effect that support for independent, samizdat or exile publications, and translations, could have in countries where culture and politics were so closely intertwined, and where the monopoly of information was such an important part of the communist parties' monopoly of power. Nonetheless, we were both sincere and consistent in taking as our first criterion intellectual and literary quality rather than putative political effect.

While support for work in Russian and German was not ruled out, we decided to concentrate our efforts on East Central Europe – Poland, Hungary, Czechoslovakia – as well as considering work in or from "smaller" languages of South Eastern and Eastern Europe. What after 1990 would become the countries of the "Visegrad group" – and "Central Europe" in the new political shorthand of the West – remained the main focus of our activities. It was here that we undoubtedly developed the greatest expertise. After 1990, however, we did extend our activities quite vigorously to Romania and Bulgaria, and, to a lesser extent, to the Baltic states.

Two other aspects of our work are reflected in the minutes of that first meeting. Firstly, as a group of authors, scholars and publishers we immediately started talking about the merits of individual titles and journals: the works of Thomas Masaryk, the Hungarian historian Jeno Szucs, the journal *Cross Currents*, and so on. This detailed consideration of the intellectual merits of individual works was, I believe, one of our distinguishing features and greatest strengths.

Secondly, we started looking for a more attractive name than the cumbersome "Central and East European Publishing Project". "ERASMUS? ECHO? CONCORDE?" note the minutes. This search for a more catchy name would continue for several years, and in the end become a standing joke among us. "The committee tried and tried but could not think of a pretty name for the CEEPP (which looks like something the Russians suggested)" record the minutes of our second meeting. The EC rapidly appropriated most of our classical ideas, for its own diverse programmes. The problem with using the names of individual great authors or places was that none of them stood for the whole of Central Europe, let alone Central and Eastern Europe: they were specifically Czech, Polish, Romanian or whatever. Finally, we came up with *Imprimatur*. But somehow it never caught on; and we went on being CEEPP (pronounced "seep") or, more colloquially, "the Oxford Project".

That last label reflected an arrangement which emerged in our first year. While the initial organisation of the Project was ably undertaken by the European Cooperation Fund in Brussels, I was then entrusted by the committee with exploring the best way to proceed. For practical reasons, it became clear that the best thing would be to open an office in Oxford. In the autumn of 1986, this was duly established, in modest premises above a junk shop in East Oxford. Our visitors, even those from the poorest corners of Eastern Europe, certainly never felt overawed by our office there. They also understood that the money really was intended to go to them, not to bureaucracy or intermediaries. At the same time, we were very fortunate to enlist the services of Elizabeth Winter, a specialist in Russian and East European literature and assistant editor at the *Times Literary Supplement*, as Project Director. Formally speaking, the Project became a UK-registered charity in early 1987, but that change scarcely affected either the substance or, let it be stressed, the all-European nature of our work.

The substance of our work was further defined at our second meeting in terms of two main headings: "continued publication" (in Polish, Hungarian, Czech, etc.) and "improved translation" (from, into and between those languages).

## Continued publication

"Continued publication" meant different things in different countries. Even before 1989, much work of real quality and critical content could be published officially in Hungary. Czechoslovakia was the other extreme. "Vaclav Havel put it very starkly" (my report to our June 1986 meeting notes). "'Without the Czech periodicals and book publishers in the West,'" he said, "'contemporary Czech literature would cease to exist.'" The hope for the future of Czech culture lay with samizdat and exile publications. Poland, by contrast, had a remarkably vigorous publishing sector in all three categories: samizdat, exile and official.

Our task was both simplified and complicated by the fact that there already existed "intermediary" organisations set up by Czech or Polish exiles to help the embattled cultures of their own lands. In the pre-1989 period, it clearly made sense to channel a significant part of our aid through them. Thus the minutes record major grants to the Fund for the Continuity of Independent Polish Literature and Humanities, an organisation which brought together distinguished Polish writers, editors and literary critics under the chairmanship of Czeslaw Milosz, the Nobel Prize-winning poet. We could hardly do better than them in selecting Polish titles worthy of support.

For what was then still Czechoslovakia, we supported a number of activities of the Czechoslovak Documentation Centre for the Promotion of Independent Literature. A remarkable initiative by the historian Vilem Precan, this Centre had been given a home by the Czech-speaking Prince Karl (or Karel) Schwarzenberg in one of his castles, at Scheinfeld in Bavaria. Not only did the Centre build up a unique collection of Czech samizdat, meticulously catalogued under Dr Precan's supervision: a treasure trove for future historians. It was also a centre for intensive secret communications with the banned and persecuted intellectuals in Czechoslovakia itself. I remember Vilem Precan once proudly showing me a video which had been sent him by Vaclav Havel. It recorded a kind of riotous fancy dress picnic somewhere in the Czech countryside, in the middle of which a ridiculously old-fashioned postman came bicycling in, ringing his bell and crying "Message from Precan!".

He might also have been crying "Message from Janouch!" or "Message from Kavan!", for both the Stockholm-based Charta 77 Foundation, run by the tireless exiled physicist Frantisek Janouch, and the London-based Palach Press and Jan Palach Information and Research Trust, run by the equally indefatigable Jan Kavan, performed a similar combination of support for exile and samizdat publications, and courier services for the embattled intellectuals. For several years we underwrote, in particular, the Charta 77 Foundation programme for Czech and Slovak books. Such support from exile-led groups is often controversial, and we found ourselves playing host, at one memorable lunch, to a vigorous exchange of views between the chairman of the foundation and his own panel of literary advisers.

The often thankless work of the emigré activist requires (and perhaps also helps to produce) a certain kind of personality, not without sharp edges. Yet their work certainly deserves an honourable place in the history of the preservation of independent Czech and Slovak culture against the best efforts of the "President of Forgetting", Gustav Husak.

Nonetheless, where we felt we had the knowledge and specialist advice to make our own decisions directly, title by title, we were glad to do so. This involved discussing individual publishers' budgets and deciding, for example, whether an item laconically labelled "*Schmuggel*" was excessive or not. It also involved lively discussion of the merits of individual titles. One of the most impressive publisher's lists we supported directly, over several years, was that of the Toronto-based Czech-language 68 Publishers, run by the writer Josef Skvorecky and his wife Zdenka Salivarova. I wonder how many readers of Skvorecky's own novels had any inkling of his services to Czech culture as a publisher. The catalogue list below gives some idea of the range and diversity of individual book titles we supported.

At the same time, we were particularly conscious of the important role played by journals in this part of Europe, a phenomenon to which Milan Kundera had recently drawn the attention of a wider Western readership in his influential essay on "The tragedy of Central Europe". Once again, this catalogue list indicates the range of journals we helped keep alive, as well as giving a short description of each. Three Polish journals indicate the different kinds of enterprise involved, and the particular challenges involved with each.

*Krytyka* was one of the leading platforms for intellectual debate among the "secular left" part of the broad Solidarity tradition, its most prominent editor being Adam Michnik. As Michnik wrote in a letter soliciting support from the West: "despite 'glasnost' there is no substitute for a free press". *Krytyka* was at this time a purely samizdat quarterly, produced in conspiratorial conditions on relatively crude offset presses. The secret police kept a close eye on its leading luminaries. Our first support was therefore given in cash, in dollar bills of relatively small denominations, which I handed over conspiratorially to Adam Michnik on one of my trips to Poland. Our files contain my formal certification for this necessarily somewhat informal transaction.

*Res Publica* had been a samizdat journal, like *Krytyka*, but of a liberal conservative orientation. In late 1986 its leading light, the historian and commentator Marcin Krol, decided to try to explore what he saw to be a new opening in Polish politics following an amnesty for political prisoners, by attempting to bring out *Res Publica* as a legal publication. This possibility he explored over an elaborate lunch with the notorious spokesman for the Jaruzelski regime, Jerzy Urban: an experiment in "supping with the devil" which was not universally applauded among the underground and opposition activists at the time.

Nonetheless, it did the trick, and our files contain a copy of the permit from the censor's office for the publication of this journal, in 25,000 copies: "subject area – the cultural and social problematic taking account of the links between Polish Christian and humanist traditions and the present." There follows a tortuous correspondence between the Project and the editors about how exactly to make a legal transfer of our grant to help pay for typesetting and photocopying equipment. "Polish bank accepts without any problems only cheques issued by Barclays Bank," writes Marcin Krol, "all others are sent back and so on and it takes about three months." And he concludes charmingly: "I'm very sorry for all inconveniences that we create, but 'socialist' countries are like that." Which indeed they were.

The third example is *Zeszyty Literackie*, a literary quarterly set up in Paris by a group of writers and critics from the younger generation who found themselves in the West when General Jaruzelski declared martial law. Under the tireless and meticulous editorship of Barbara Torunczyk, *Zeszyty Literackie* did not have an explicitly political or even sociocultural programme, as *Krytyka* and *Res Publica* did. Instead, its programme was simple and resolutely aesthetic: to publish, elegantly and accurately, the very best literary writing in Polish, together with good translations of essays, poetry and prose relating to what Barbara Torunczyk delphically christened "Europe of the centre".

Her problems were different from those of her contemporaries and friends in Warsaw. *Zeszyty* could be, and was, designed, typeset and produced to the highest standards. Communications were easy, and financial transfers could be made by the regular channels. But there was all the loneliness and insecurity of exile, while for a journal to survive and function in the expensive, hard-currency West, with many of its readers in the soft-currency East, demanded larger sums than were needed by journals inside Poland. I think Barbara Torunczyk would testify that CEEPP's regular annual grants made a very significant contribution to keeping *Zeszyty* alive through the seven lean years of exile – although of course, there were other generous contributors, including many from individual readers. It was a source of deep satisfaction to all of us that *Zeszyty Literackie* was subsequently able to make a gradual transition back to Warsaw, where it now continues to flourish as Poland's best literary quarterly.

I have dwelt on the story of these three Polish journals not only because it is one I know especially well but also because it nicely illustrates the diversity of Central and East European publishing at this time. In the Hungarian case, official cultural journals were generally subsidised by the state, as part of what Miklos Haraszti has called the intellectuals' "velvet prison". Yet just for that reason, an important role was played by the much less numerous samizdat journals, such as

*Beszelo* and *Hirmondo*, as well as those, like *Magyar Fuzetek*, produced by Hungarians in exile.

In Czechoslovakia, the official journals could virtually be discounted, but there was a rich and flourishing world of samizdat and exile journals. I remember with particular pleasure a trip Elizabeth Winter and I made in the early summer of 1989 to meet a group of Czech samizdat editors in Budapest. The exiled Czech writer Jiri Grusa had rented a discreet chalet apartment in the wooded grounds of a quiet motel. In a scene worthy of a Soviet propaganda film about Western imperialist spies, we produced wads of dollar bills from our coat pockets, counting out $1,000 to *Vokno*, $2,000 to *O Divadle*, $1,000 to *Paraf*, and so on. One of the liveliest literary journals, *Revolver Revue*, decided they wanted equipment instead. In October 1989, Elizabeth Winter and Sally Laird visited Prague to follow up on this and other Czechoslovak requests. Sally Laird recalls: "We spent a lot of time in telephone boxes with fistfuls of small change, and Liz assumed a mysterious accent when making veiled enquiries over the phone. At Eda Kriseova's we all spoke in Russian. I imagine the listeners-in must have been rather baffled, though they must have been familiar with the imperial tongue."

The last act of this particular play took place in the midst of the "velvet revolution", in November 1989, when I participated in a hurried meeting with Vaclav Havel, Karl Schwarzenberg, Frantisek Janouch and the editors of *Revolver Revue* huddled round a table in a shabby backroom, all empty beer cans and full ashtrays. But the $10,000 CEEPP voted for equipment for *Revolver Revue* was finally transferred to them in a quite new world, the world after the velvet revolutions. No more furtive backward glances as one slipped into apartment buildings; no more addresses concealed on the backs of Eurocheques; no more wads of dollar bills: goodbye to all that!

## Improved translation

So far as "improved translation" was concerned, we started by making extensive enquiries to establish which major works, in what might broadly be described as the modern humanities, had been translated from these languages into the major Western languages; who was available to translate such works; and, most important of all, what deserved to be translated but had not been. To assist in the first task, we commissioned a report from the Polish scholar Jakub Karpinski on "Central European literature in the West". To assist in the second, Zsuzsa Szabo prepared a bibliographical report on "Central European literary translators and translations". To assist in the third, we wrote to a number of leading editors, writers and scholars for suggestions.

These two excellent reports and the detailed responses to our letter formed the base on which we built constantly through our own enquiries and contacts. I still have the small black notebook in which I scribbled down these often excited suggestions in the corner of some dim café in Prague or Budapest. Increasingly, as the Project became better known, people volunteered their own further suggestions.

We did not naively assume that there were infinite riches awaiting translators. In my report, I quoted Havel once again, this time warning against "the patriotic illusion that the world, due to its invincible ignorance, remains deprived of some fabulous intellectual achievements waiting here on every corner". Moreover, quite a few books which were praised to us in glowing terms, by the local critics in the dim cafés, turned out on closer examination, in the brighter, cooler light of a sample translation, to be derivative, self-referential, hopelessly allusive, unbearably prolix, or simply not to work in translation. This applied particularly to books which had been written with the hope of official publication. In order to smuggle their message past the censor, writers often resorted to the "Aesopian" techniques of concealed allusion, allegory or fable. But what defeated the censor often also defeated the translator, or at least, the Western reader who had to make sense of the translation.

A fair amount of our effort thus consisted in establishing what was *not* going to work in translation, and, with time, our drawers were filled with such sample translations. Over the years we did, nonetheless, find quite a number of books that richly deserved a wider readership, and even a few buried treasures, of which more below.

As I have mentioned already, we discussed each individual translation proposal on its own intellectual and literary merits. We also carefully scrutinised the publishers' budgets, which in some cases would themselves have earned a place in the fiction lists. If the book looked worthwhile, and the budget serious, we generally tried to earmark our contribution for the translation costs. Once again, the catalogue that follows gives an idea of the extraordinarily wide range of translations at whose birth we assisted.

One particular feature of this earlier period deserves to be stressed: the relatively large number of books translated from one Central or East European language to another. This was a conscious priority, reflecting the hopes of the "Central European" debate at the time that these countries would look to and learn from each other, and not just each, individually, stare westward. Brodsky in Czech, Eliade in Polish, Michnik in Hungarian, Konrad and Kolakowski in Bulgarian, Starobinski in Serbo-Croat, all were to serve that noble, idealistic purpose. It is a sad though not a surprising fact that the interest in such translations declined rather rapidly after 1989.

Of course we also supported a number of translations from Western into Central and East European languages. One of the greatest problems Central and East European publishers encountered here was the copyright fees demanded by Western authors or their agents in hard currency which those publishers did not possess. Sometimes we helped them to pay these, but we also tried on occasion to appeal to the goodwill of the authors, with some success. Significantly less success was had with one or two of the more grasping literary agents who operated in the region.

We were naturally interested not just in the translations but also in the translators. It hardly needed our report on translators to emphasise to us the lonely, underpaid condition under which most translators worked; and, of course, not just those working from or into these languages. In order to do major work well they obviously needed both adequate financial support and, ideally, conditions in which they could discuss that work with sympathetic and qualified colleagues. We therefore considered very early in the day the idea of establishing a "translators' fellowship". We found an ideal partner for this enterprise in the Institute for Human Sciences in Vienna. Founded by a young Polish philosopher in the early 1980s, with the benign patronage of the Pope, but by no means committed to Catholic dogma, this Institute had already by 1986 become a unique place for intellectuals from Eastern and Western Europe to meet and work together.

In early 1987 we gave our first grant to help establish the "translators' fellowship" there, and then supported it continuously until 1994. In fact, at our very last meeting we gave a further grant to help the programme continue after we had gone. The fruits of this programme are described in the following catalogue.

As in the field of "continued publication" so also in that of "improved translation" we found that the role of journals was crucial. From the very beginning we were delighted to support *Cross Currents*, a pioneering yearbook produced almost single handedly by the exiled Czech critic Ladislav Matejka, at the University of Michigan. This brought previously unknown Central European writers and artists to an interested audience in the English-speaking world, and especially in North America. *Lettre Internationale* was (and remains) a remarkable attempt by the dynamic Czech editor Antonin Liehm to produce a genuinely pan-European intellectual review to rival the *New York Review of Books*. *East European Reporter* and *Labour Focus on Eastern Europe* were invaluable sources of detailed, up-to-date information on political, social and economic developments behind the iron curtain. *L'Autre Europe* provided more reflective and scholarly analysis for a French-speaking readership.

Arien Mack, the editor of the New York-based quarterly *Social Research*, told us she would like to "return to the [journal's] East European roots" by devoting one special issue a year to Central and East European social thought and research. This she proceeded to do, with our financial help, and the resulting series of special issues has become a valuable resource for the study of the region as well as providing many Central and East European scholars with the opportunity, and the discipline, of publishing in English. Arien Mack's contacts with her Central and East European contributors subsequently inspired her to organise, with great vigour and self-sacrifice, a most impressive programme for supplying Western journals free to Central and East European libraries.

One particular gap we noted early on was the lack of a serious journal in the German language which would regularly bring the cultural and intellectual debates of Central and Eastern Europe to German readers in their original form. This seemed particularly regrettable in view of the rapidly growing importance which West Germany and, to a lesser extent, Austria, were now again assuming in the area. The intellectual proponents of a new "*Mitteleuropa*" and a new "*Stredni Evropa*" or "*Europa Srodkowa*" were talking a lot about each other, but much less to each other.

Here we once again found an ideal partner in the Institute for Human Sciences. Together with us and the *Neue Kritik* publishing house in Frankfurt, Krzysztof Michalski and Klaus Nellen developed the concept for a new journal, on whose editorial or advisory boards several of us joined in our, so to speak, explicitly intellectual capacity. We chose the title *Transit*: a word with many meanings, all of them appropriate to a journal which aimed to be a regular intellectual forum for scholars and writers from East and West. By the time the first issue was actually produced, in 1990, the title had acquired a further meaning: transit from communism. But would that also, necessarily, be transit to democracy?

## AFTER (1990–1994)

In the euphoria of late 1989 and early 1990, many people in Poland, Hungary and Czechslovakia fondly hoped that their countries would experience a rapid and relatively painless transition to normality, prosperity, democracy, the rule of law, pluralism and the West. All these things were somehow believed to go easily, even automatically, together, and all were summed up in one phrase: "the return to Europe".

Ralf Dahrendorf, in his *Reflections on the Revolution in Europe*, was one of the first to warn that the transition would be longer and more painful than many might hope, and that even in the West the relationship between these different facets of "normality" was more complex than many imagined. Others, myself included, tried to ensure that the west, north and south European political and economic entity which bore the name "Europe" now lived up to that name, by responding with generosity of spirit, open frontiers and (not least) open markets to the other Europeans now longing to join.

Meanwhile, we were confronted with the question of how our small Project could best contribute to this larger, indeed this huge and daunting historic task. We seriously considered whether we should not simply close down, on the grounds that in the field of publishing something approaching a European "normality" should be achievable in a relatively short period, and that a wholly new situation required a new way of working. Cries of dismay from our grantees, advisers and, indeed, most of our own trustees, soon taught us otherwise. Moreover, already in 1990 it was clear that the transition would be painful, and that in the short term things might actually get worse rather than better. We nonetheless took the firm decision to work towards our own extinction. After all, the ultimate success for the Project would be for it to have become superfluous.

Initially, we decided to continue for another three years. In 1991, in consultation with our major funders, we decided to work towards close-down at the end of 1994, while appointing three new Central European trustees to increase our direct presence and expertise in our main area of activity. In December 1991 we were delighted to welcome the Hungarian philosopher Gyorgy Bence, the Polish historian Jerzy Jedlicki, and the Czech writer Eda Kriseova to our board.

A year later several of our trustees, and Laurens van Krevelen in particular, felt that there would still be important work to be done after

1994. Together with Raymond Georis, he therefore set up in early 1993 what became the Dutch Fund for Central and East European Book Projects. This ran in parallel with CEEPP for nearly two years, making separate grants but with the board of trustees in fact being identical, before taking on its own fully independent life after the end of CEEPP.

The great change of 1989/90 also coincided with some lesser changes in the organisation of the Oxford office. In early 1990 the office itself moved from East Oxford to more salubrious premises in the St Antony's College annexe. From here, those working for the Project could draw on the considerable human and scholarly resources of the College, with its long tradition of studying Central and Eastern Europe. They could also be in close touch with the Soros office, based in the same building. Visitors to one would often drop into the other. George Soros himself had generously supported the work of the Project in its early years, through his Open Society Fund, and our workshop on journals, of which more below, was jointly organised with the Soros Foundations.

In the second half of 1989, Elizabeth Winter stepped down as Project Director, while continuing as Secretary to the Trustees, and we were very lucky to find Sally Laird, formerly editor of *Index on Censorship*, as our new Project Director. To complete the changes, Alison Oldfield, our highly efficient first assistant director, decided to move on to other things, and Maria Williamson succeeded her, bringing not only secretarial skills but also knowledge of her native tongue, Czech. When Sally Laird had to move to Denmark at the beginning of 1993, Elizabeth Winter returned as Project Director, while Danuta Garton Ash, who had already been working as the Polish reader for the Project, became more closely involved as a Consultant.

What we did in the last five years of our activity was in some respects quite different from what we had done in the first four. Yet it still fell broadly into our two main categories of "continued publication" and "improved translation". It is under these headings that I shall attempt to outline and illustrate our work in the years "after", before concluding with a brief assessment of the Project as a whole.

## Continued publication

There were, it will be clear, three different broad categories of publishers and journals involved in the transition: official, samizdat and exile. All faced the raw wind of a market made more cruel by specific problems of transition such as the collapse of central, state-owned distribution systems, soaring printing and paper costs, the relative impoverishment of the intelligentsia – the main book-buying class – and the new competition of other forms of entertainment, such as videos and computer games. All had to decide whether to boost their income by venturing, albeit somewhat sheepishly – perhaps under another imprint – into the boom areas of English-language and business textbooks, thrillers, cookbooks or soft porn. All had to discover whole new dimensions of the publishing business: marketing and promotion, for example. All had to cope with pirates at every stage of the publishing process.

Beyond this, however, their problems were different. The official publishing houses had been classic communist state enterprises, with large, direct subsidies from the state, no notion of profit or loss, free or artificially low-rent premises in prime locations, and, above all, huge numbers of editorial staff. Where a Western publisher producing a roughly equivalent list might have had 20 editors, they had 100. The rapid move to the free market, including the slashing of state subsidies, plunged them into crisis, to which some responded successfully while others went under. The underground publishers and journals had the opposite problem: no infrastructure, no premises, no equipment, no staff. Finally, the exile publishers and journal editors faced the truly existential question of whether, and if so how, to return to the countries in which they had never expected to be able to live again.

These problems were plainly of a quite different kind, and, in particular, of a different financial dimension, from those we had addressed before 1989. At the same time, much larger Western "players", to use the jargon of the international policy trade, were advancing into the field: the (then still) EC, and the group of 24 states whose aid it coordinated; the national aid programmes, such as the British Know-How Fund or the American National Endowment for Democracy; the German party foundations, who until then had been distinguished by their extreme and indeed programmatic timidity in dealing with anything "oppositional" in Soviet-controlled Europe; George Soros with his Soros Foundations, on a larger scale than before; even the World Bank.

We decided to concentrate on a limited number of tasks. First, we gave direct, targeted help to those formerly underground or exiled independent publishers and journals whose track record we knew and whose needs were pressing and immediate. In my view, this was probably the most important thing the Project, specifically, did in 1990 and 1991. In particular, we gave a whole series of grants for the basic equipment (computers, typesetting machines, photocopiers) urgently needed by smaller independent publishers or journals to establish themselves in the new conditions. In Poland these included the well-known samizdat houses of *Nowa* and *Krag* as well as the independent, liberal Catholic house of *Znak*; journals such as *Krytyka*, of the left, *Arka*, of the right, and *Brulion*, an organ of angry young writers, as well as the book programme of *Res Publica*. For Czechoslovakia there was a particularly long list, including *Lidove noviny*, a samizdat journal which was to become one of the country's leading newspapers, *Revolver Revue*, *Stredni Evropa*, *Most*, *150,000 Slov*, *Prostor* and such publishing houses as *Archa*, *Atlantis* and *Torst*.

We had not previously spent so much money in Hungary, where the pre-1989 needs were less acute, but were now glad to be able to give a helping hand to a wide range of very interesting Hungarian journals, including the new Budapest Review of Books, *Buksz*, the high quality literary journal *Holmi*, *Nappali haz*, smaller journals such as *Gond* as well as a number of individual book titles from the lists of dynamic new independent publishers such as *Szazadveg*, which grew out of a student magazine, and *Atlantisz*. Again, full titles are to be found in the catalogue, but I mention a few here to show the range and also to indicate, for those who know the houses and journals in question, that our criterion was quality, not political orientation, milieu or clique.

We were especially happy to assist in the return of exiled publications, publishers and institutions to the home country. I have mentioned already one of the most spectacularly successful of these: that of the Polish literary quarterly *Zeszyty Literackie* from Paris to Warsaw. But it was equally satisfying to see the London-based Polish publishers *Aneks* coming forward with applications for what in the end would be four volumes of previously unpublished Politburo documents, giving fascinating insights into the history of communist Poland, and now published and distributed by *Aneks* in Poland as well as in the West. Or the previously England-based Czech publisher, *Rozmluvy*, publishing a massive revisionist history of Czechoslovakia, prepared in extremely difficult "underground" conditions by a team of banned historians led by Petr Pithart – who in the meantime had become Czech Prime Minister. Or Vilem Precan applying in his new guise as Director of a new Institute for Contemporary History in Prague. The list could be continued.

Under this general heading of "return" one should also mention the exiled authors whose "returns" into their native languages we helped to support: Leszek Kolakowski on the *Main Currents of Marxism*, "back" into his native Polish; Istvan Deak on the Austro-Hungarian officer corps, "back" into his native Hungarian; Jacques Rupnik on *The Other Europe*, "back" into his native Czech; and so on. They occupied an important intermediate (and intermediary) place between the local authors and the Western authors whose work it was only now possible to publish legally, not just in samizdat or exile translations.

A second distinguishing feature of our work in the post-1990 period was a geographical extension to include, particularly, more emphasis on Bulgaria and Romania, and to a lesser extent on the Baltic states. Here the financial needs were still more acute, and the transition to cultural pluralism and full freedom of expression less self-evident. In the case of Romania, in particular, Sally Laird found both the old spirit of heavy-handed central control and a new chaos haunting the eerie Stalinist ziggurat now known as the House of the Free Press. While the poet-revolutionary Mircea Dinescu preached a "democracy of cafés", in practice he wanted aid to be channelled through his Union of Writers.

This we did not do, but instead gave direct subsidies to a number of struggling independent journals, such as *Twenty Two*, *Contrapunct* and *Interval*, and to those publishers, like *Humanitas*, who were striving to be both genuinely liberal and independent.

Similarly in Bulgaria, we supported the work of independent journals, such as *Panorama*, *Izbor* and *Political Studies*, and specific book titles from the lists of the more enterprising quality publishers. Our contribution was relatively small in size, but then so was Bulgaria's liberal intelligentsia. Several of its leading figures became good friends, spending extended periods in Oxford on their own account. Sally Laird's visits, and our support, did, I know, do something to remedy the feeling, quite widespread in Bulgaria and Romania, that the West was showing too much favouritism to what had by 1993 become the "Visegrad Four". Yet there is no denying the fact that the Oxford Project's main focus, and main expertise, remained in what Western politicians had now increasingly learned to call Central Europe.

Beyond this direct action, however, we decided to make a major effort to help bring "know-how" in the broadest sense to book publishers and journal editors. In this, we were of course not alone. Peter Kaufman's New York-based *Pubwatch* organisation, in particular, has made an impressive contribution in this respect since its foundation in 1990. One of the things we did was therefore to bring together as many representatives as possible of organisations supporting publishing in the region, to discuss with a select group of Central and East European publishers how Western help could best be coordinated and directed. Some sixty people attended what was emphatically not just another conference but a working meeting, a genuine workshop, at St Antony's College in November 1991.

A full report was issued and circulated at the time, and a summary is included in the catalogue below, but among the points that emerged I might single out four. A common litany of complaints from all the Central and East European publishers concerned the problems of distribution. It was interesting to hear the wide variety of proposals from the Western side for addressing the problem, ranging from a multi-million dollar sectoral scheme being developed under World Bank auspices to the modest proposal from Jessica Douglas-Home of the Eminescu Trust – that someone should simply go out and buy a van for a Romanian publisher. I think it fair to say that the latter proposal was greeted with more real enthusiasm by our Central and East European publishers than the former: they could imagine a van, they could also imagine the outcome of a World Bank study. But ideally the action needed would lie somewhere between these two extremes. As Richard Davy reports below, when he toured East Central Europe in 1994 this problem was still very high on the publishers' lists of problems.

There was also considerable concern about the lack of coordination between different Western programmes of support. Our workshop was itself intended as a small contribution to better coordination. We were also very pleased to join with Pubwatch and the (British) Publishers' Association in producing a *Directory of Western Organisations Assisting Book Culture in Central and Eastern Europe and the Former Soviet Union.*

Thirdly, there was interesting discussion of where subsidies went in a "normal" West European or North American publishing context. The head of one leading university press pointed out that, although we do not have so many supply-side subsidies (i.e. directly to publishers), we have very substantial demand-side subsidies, through public budgets for libraries, universities and student grants. Without these, he argued, academic publishing could hardly exist. In the longer term, it was felt this was an aspect of publishing "normality" to which Central and East European countries might also wish to aspire. But where was the money to come from, given the crisis of all their state budgets? Perhaps Western donors could help here, through independent local bodies of an "arts council" type? The suggestion is further explored in Richard Davy's chapter below.

Finally, several of the Central and East European publishers present suggested that the best help they could receive would not be direct grants or even visiting experts, but the chance to see for themselves, at first hand, how Western publishers work. This was a suggestion which we took up and pursued, working jointly with the Publishers Association. The result was a programme of publishing "internships", known formally as the Senior Managers' Attachment Programme, in which editors or managers from Central and East European publishing houses came for a carefully designed visit of between one and three weeks with a British publisher.

The visitors, who were carefully selected by a joint CEEPP–Publishers Association committee, came from a wide variety of publishing houses, state, independent and formerly underground, large and small, literary, general and academic, and the attempt was made to place them with a roughly equivalent house in Britain. In all, 19 Central and East European publishers came to Britain on this programme in the years 1992–94, and a further 21 on a group visit to the London Book Fair in 1994.

The final reports submitted by the visiting publishers bear witness to the value of this exercise. "This method of training works ... I have already introduced changes based on the Chapman & Hall solutions", wrote Michal Szewileow of the Polish publisher PWN. Janos Gyurgyak, the dynamic Hungarian editor and publisher from Szazadveg, was impressed by the degree to which decisions were made collectively in the publishing house to which he was attached: "that kind of collective work was a surprise for me coming from a former 'collective', socialist (or what) country." He praised the personal contacts made, and stressed the value of what he had learned about marketing, in particular: "After I had returned home I reorganised my publishing house (established a marketing department, etc.)." We are particularly glad that the Publishers Association will be continuing this programme after 1994.

In January 1993 we organised another workshop, also held at St Antony's, on "The Future of Journals in Central and Eastern Europe". This we co-hosted with the *Times Literary Supplement* – the TLS – which also offered free subscription and advertising space to the participating journals. A remarkable assemblage of journal editors and publishers descended on Oxford from every corner of Central and Eastern Europe, from Albania to Lithuania, together with a few editors from Western Europe, and the representatives of many funders and, notably, most of the Soros Foundations. A summary is given below, but a few points may again be singled out.

As at the publishing workshop, there was an interesting discussion of what in fact constitutes publishing "normality" in the West. It rapidly emerged that this normality, or rather, the varieties of differing national "normalities", are quite far removed from the ideal type of the pure free market so energetically preached by the West to the post-communist East. To be sure, much could be learned from a dynamic and commercially successful literary journal like *Granta*, from whose Deputy Editor we heard about subscription promotion schemes, market research, targeted mail shots, and the like. But there are obviously journals of poetry, for example, which can only survive with direct subsidy. Others, such as scholarly journals, are carried as part of a larger stable in the journals department of a book publishing house; others again rely on a single rich individual the patron or "sugar daddy".

Turning to the current position of journals in Central and Eastern Europe, we had a very interesting range of contributions from editors of journals from Vilnius to Brasov, and Prague to Belgrade. All reflected on the traumas of change and what Henryk Wozniakowski of the Polish journal *Znak* called "the inflation of the free word". This recalled to my mind Philip Roth's pithy observation after a trip to Prague before 1989. He returned, said Roth, with the impression that whereas in the West everything goes and nothing matters, in the East nothing goes and everything matters. Now, by these accounts, the East was in this respect all too rapidly joining the West. "Who needs culture any more?" was the despairing cry of Gheorghe Craciun from the Transylvanian journal *Interval*.

Summarising his impression of this discussion, George Soros suggested that the question "From dissidence to what?" might be answered as "From dissidence to dissidence". Except, insisted an editor of *Revolver Revue*, that they no longer felt an urgent moral obligation to indulge in politics, in the sense of criticising the powers-that-be. And what a relief, what a genuine liberation that was!

This interesting intellectual debate was brought down to earth by a Romanian editor who observed bluntly: "The main problem is the lack of money." The practical discussions which followed were not, however, devoted simply to that. A working group on direct subsidy also considered the question of accountability. Another working group considered the problems of distribution, as acute for journals as for books. A third considered possibilities of international cooperation. One idea that received strong support in this group was that of a "journal of journals" or "review of reviews": the idea being that participating journals could receive a short summary of what other journals across Europe were publishing, together with information about how translation rights could be obtained.

An excellent idea, we thought, and one which we subsequently tried to follow up, circulating all the participating journals, and quite a few more, with a concrete proposal. All they had to do was to send us their own contents summaries; we would put them into a common format, and circulate the complete set to all who had contributed. The response was extremely disappointing, and we decided in the end that there was not sufficient commitment from a sufficient number of journals to make it worthwhile. Not for the first time, one was confronted with the gulf between theory and practice in the intellectual life of Central and Eastern Europe.

Nonetheless, we had enthusiastic responses from many of those who participated in the workshop. As so often with conferences or workshops, a good part of the value lay in the informal, personal contacts made and the discussions "in the margins". Particularly so in this case because, in contrast with many international conferences, those who met here were not people who meet each other all the time, travelling from conference to conference. A high proportion of them, even of those from Central European neighbours such as Poland and the Czech Republic, were meeting each other for the first time. It is perhaps ironical but also, alas, all too typical, that editors from Prague had to come to Oxford to meet editors from Warsaw, not to mention those from Tirana and Sofia, Belgrade and Budapest.

## Improved translation

In the post-1990 period there was an even larger overlap than before between "continued publication" and "improved translation". Much of what has been mentioned in the previous section had a major element of translation and dissemination: the journals, obviously, and the "return" of Central and East European authors to publication in their native languages. There was also the continuation of a major part of our, so to speak, bread-and-butter work at the trustees' meetings: the scrutiny of individual translation proposals from individual publishers, and the award of grants for the translation of designated titles, on the basis of the quality of the work to be translated, the seriousness of the publisher making the proposal, and the realism of the budget submitted. Again, the wide range of titles supported can be seen from the following catalogue.

We continued to support a few selected journals bringing Central and East European literature, politics and scholarly debate to audiences in Western languages. These included the German language *Transit*, *Cross Currents* and further special issues of *Social Research*, but also such new departures as *Trafika*. This is a journal of international writing produced in Prague by some of those young Westerners, and notably Americans, who have been endeavouring to reproduce in the Prague of the 1990s something of the Paris of the 1920s. Whether their number will include a new Hemingway or Joyce remains to be seen.

As mentioned above, we continued to support the Translation Fellowship programme at the Institute for Human Sciences in Vienna, and Elizabeth Winter regularly participated in their selection committee meetings. A list of those who benefitted, and the books they worked on, can be found in the catalogue below. In June 1994 our Dutch sister-trust organised a workshop for literary translators in Oestgeest, Holland, which is also briefly summarised below. They will now be trying to put some of its lessons into practice.

So far as the Oxford Project is concerned, two special new emphases need to be mentioned. One is the significant number of Western texts, especially in political philosophy, history, economics, psychology and social thought, for the translation of which into one or other Central or East European language our support was requested. There was a veritable flood of such requests after 1990, reflecting the desire to catch up with what had been written and debated in the West for the fifty years in which countries had been cut off from it. We were delighted to support these translation proposals where they seemed to us worthwhile (see the catalogue list), but we did notice that a number of names kept recurring again and again – Hayek, Popper, Orwell, Arendt – while others, who had in fact had a profound influence in the West, hardly appeared at all.

Our list of "100 Books which have influenced Western public discourse since the Second World War", included at the end of this volume is, in part, a response to those numerous Central and East European publishers' lists that we scrutinised at successive meetings, and in part a response to direct requests that we have received, individually or collectively, for such recommendations. (In particular, we have been interested to hear of the Central European University Press's ambitious programme for translating basic works essential to an understanding of the open society into all the languages of Central and Eastern Europe.) Self-evidently this selection of "100 books" is a highly arbitrary exercise, indeed a *jeu d'esprit*. Yet certainly there are a number of titles on the list which almost nobody in Central or Eastern Europe will have heard of, but which had a considerable influence on the evolution of Western public discourse.

Even if intellectuals from the former West and the former East in Europe have arrived at more or less the same point – that is, one or other version of liberalism – they have done so by very different routes. Our *jeu d'esprit* is informed by the serious conviction that in order to understand each other fully we have to know not only "where we're at" but also "where we're coming from", to use the American colloquial phrases. This list, in all its diversity of subject, direction and, indeed, true intellectual quality, is also an account of where we, from the West, are coming from. Nonetheless, conscious of the arbitrariness of the exercise, we should of course be happy for readers to add to our list their own "missing persons".

The second CEEPP initiative in the field of translation which deserves special mention is the series of Central European Classics. The origins of this series go back to the very beginning of the Project, when I started that hunt for the "buried treasure" of Central European literature, noting down titles in the dim cafés. Our original wish was very much to take these works, when found, "out of the ghetto": that is, onto the general lists of mainstream publishers. In some cases we succeeded, but in many it proved almost impossible, even with the offer of a direct translation subsidy. This was especially true of pre-1945 literature. Contemporary fiction was obviously seen to have more "sex appeal", particularly if there had recently been a Soviet invasion of the country from which the author came. Thus English-speaking readers had access to the works of Kundera, Skvorecky and Hrabal, but knew nothing of the literary tradition from which they came. This was like reading Grass and Böll while being totally ignorant of Mann, Döblin and Fontane.

We therefore decided to take the initiative ourselves, to try and fill this particular black hole in the literary consciousness of the West. The trustees asked me to become General Editor of a series of Central European Classics, which would aim to produce first-rate translations of works of fiction acknowledged as classics in their own countries, with introductions by contemporary Central European writers. The series was to be placed, in the first instance, with a quality English-language publisher; although it was hoped that some, at least, of the volumes might subsequently be taken up in other languages.

The organisation and coordination of publisher, translators and introducers was a demanding business, but the first two volumes in the series were elegantly published by Chatto & Windus in 1993. These were a new version of Jan Neruda's *Prague Tales*, translated by Michael Henry Heim with a vivid introduction by Ivan Klima, and the first ever translation into English of a truly wonderful novella by the Hungarian Thomas Mann: Dezso Kosztolanyi. His *Skylark*, beautifully translated by Richard Aczel and with a characteristically lively and idiosyncratic introduction by one of Hungary's leading contemporary writers, Peter Esterhazy, was a real discovery.

The critical reception in Britain was gratifying. The well-known critic Victoria Glendinning, writing in *The Times*, described precisely the problem we were addressing, but also the effect we hoped to achieve. She began her review thus: "If I were thinking of reading this review, instead of writing it, I should probably proceed no further, seeing that it is about foreign fiction by authors with difficult names of whom I have never heard. Please persist. It is important." She continued: "*Skylark*, published in Hungarian in 1924, is the most original, economical and painful novel I have read in a long time." *Prague Tales* received equally enthusiastic reviews, and also appealed to the more discriminating of the now innumerable Western visitors to the golden city. Anne Applebaum commented in the *Guardian* that with this series we had "stumbled upon half a continent's worth of forgotten genius". While naturally pleased with her conclusion, I had to smile at "stumbling". As a description of years of hard searching, the verb left something to be desired.

Unfortunately, Chatto & Windus subsequently withdrew, but in the meantime we have found an outstanding new publisher, and the series will be re-launched with Stephen Vizinczey's wonderful new translation of Zsigmond Moricz's *Be Faithful Unto Death*. Several more excellent titles are in the pipeline. To oversee and support the series we have constituted a Central European Classics Trust (which is, formally speaking, the legal successor to CEEPP under British charity law), with myself as Chairman, Elizabeth Winter as continuing trustee, Danuta Garton Ash as Secretary to the Trustees, and two new trustees: the writer and columnist Neal Ascherson, who himself has long experience of Central and Eastern Europe, and the poet and critic Craig Raine.

## CONCLUSION

Let us start with the brass tacks. Although always a small operation, we nonetheless managed to raise a total of some $3.3 million from our funders over the nine years. We disbursed some $2.65 million on grants, workshops, internships and translation promotion and a further ca. $150,000 on trustees' meetings, which, as will be clear from the above, were an essential part of the decision-making and selection process. In all, we had twenty trustees' meetings, each lasting a day and a half. Even the expenditure of ca. $500,000 on office, staff and overheads cannot be counted as simply "administration", since the office was also a meeting place for visitors and a clearing house for proposals, manuscripts, ideas.

Altogether, quite a lot of our time, quite a lot of our funders' money. Since this is something in the nature of an official history, there is a danger of self-congratulation. So let me start with possible criticisms or weaknesses. Some have charged us with "cliquishness", or sticking to a too small group of grantees. Such charges are almost inevitable in this field. I would say that we were significantly less "cliquish" than most funding offices based in the countries concerned, where the local personnel are almost inevitably part and parcel of particular intelligentsia milieux and, precisely, cliques.

It is true that we supported some publications, publishers and groups repeatedly over a number of years. For reasons I have tried to explain, I believe this was a virtue, not a fault. It is true that we did not advertise our activities *urbi et orbi* and invite applications from all corners of Central and Eastern Europe. But before 1989 that was impossible, and after 1989 we would simply have been swamped with applications for funding ten times the amount we had to disburse. As it was, we probably rejected a good half of the applications that came up for discussion, which themselves had been subjected to a fairly rigorous preliminary winnowing by the Project Diector. So that is, in my view, less a criticism than a simple reflection of the way we worked, which had pros and cons like any other way of working.

The one criticism I would partially endorse is that we were not as energetic or as vigorously present in Central and Eastern Europe in our last two years as we had been before. There were various reasons for this. As Ralf Dahrendorf observes in his introduction, there is something like a natural life to the enthusiasm and commitment of people involved in a voluntary, charitable enterprise. But this fading was also a reflection of the fact that we had taken the decision to close down CEEPP and, where appropriate, pass on the baton to others. It may theoretically be possible to "wind down" and "wind up" simultaneously, but in practice it is very difficult.

Personally, I found the experience of being closely associated with an organisation which had significant sums of money to award interesting, rewarding and sobering. One big drawback was that a certain artificiality or strain could enter into personal relationships which might otherwise have been more or less purely friendships. The "more or less" is an important qualification, since, for example, the fact of being a writer who could bring particular people or situations to the attention of a wider readership in the West was also, in some sense, a distorting factor. Indeed, one could question the whole notion of "pure" friendship, in the sense that elements like status, personal wealth or power play a part in most friendships. Yet the factor "money" clearly does produce its own peculiar and not always pleasant distortions. The great compensating advantage was, of course, that one could make a material as well as a spiritual difference to some brave and talented people doing remarkable things.

So, what did we achieve? And what remains? Here I must start with the word repeated twice in the title of this book: freedom. Our work was, in the first place, a small contribution to the incremental self-liberation of East Central Europe in the late 1980s and then to the consolidation of the new freedoms after 1989. Some prefer to talk of "cultural freedom", but it is not clear exactly what the modifier "cultural" adds to (or subtracts from) the all-important noun. As I have said, from the very beginning we were well aware that our work, though not explicitly political, with, so to speak, a large "P", was eminently political in its effects. And proud of it.

At the same time, our work was a small contribution – one among many – to bringing the two halves of an artificially divided Europe closer together again. The slightly bureaucratic term often used is "cultural exchange". One could also describe it as the cultural dimension of ending the Cold War and a contribution to the goal of *sortir de*

*Yalta*. Like so much else that has been done for Europe over the last half century, the initiative and much of the money came from America. But our own committee consisted of Europeans – with the American European or European American Jane Kramer being the exception to prove the rule.

While I am not, of course, privy to the personal politics of my fellow trustees, I think I can safely say that most of us were also liberals, albeit with a small "l" and with different varieties of liberalism. This was important too. In fact, the active engagement of liberals in the direct support of liberty behind the iron curtain was less frequent and self-evident than one might like to think. In my experience, those who did most for the embattled intellectuals of Central and Eastern Europe were very often not liberals but people with strong ideological axes of their own to grind, whether fervently Catholic, Trotskyite or neo-conservative. The group around *Labour Focus on Eastern Europe* is a good example from the left, the tireless work of the British neo-conservative philosopher Roger Scruton is a good example from the right. Indeed, one of the interesting things about working in this area was the unlikely alliances it created, a feature which of course it shared with Charta 77 or Solidarity.

It seems to me a matter of elementary historical justice to give recognition where recognition is due, irrespective of political affiliations or possible ulterior motives. But this observation also raises much deeper questions about what actually takes people to the front line of the defence of liberty, and why it is that philosophically sophisticated, tolerant, sceptical (and culturally relativist?) liberals are not so often found there. That is the subject for another essay. While it would be vainglorious and simply wrong to suggest that we were in the front line of the defence of liberty, it is fair to say that in this case, at least, those parachuting in a few much-needed supplies were themselves liberals. Thus, this was the work of liberals for liberty as well as of Europeans for Europe.

What remains? Well, first of all there are the actual books and journals whose publication we supported: complete sets of them at St Antony's in Oxford and in the offices of the Dutch Fund, individual volumes in hundreds of libraries and thousands of studies, sitting-rooms, perhaps even bedrooms, across Europe and North America. Then there are the publishers, journals and translators whom we helped to keep going, perhaps a little better equipped, more knowledgeable, with contacts made through the workshops or translation fellowships, and so on. Then there are CEEPP's "successors" addressing the still unfinished business: the Dutch Fund, the Classics Trust, the internship programme being continued by the Publishers' Association, and perhaps – who knows? – some of our original funders taking up one or other suggestion made in Richard Davy's report at the end of this volume.

It might seem logical to end with that – looking to the future. Yet there is one other, less obvious element which seems to me very important, for the future as well as the past. That element is memory. Or rather, memories: the individual memories of those who participated in or benefited from the Project's work. At our last trustees' meeting, we went round the table commenting on an outline of this short history. I was particularly struck by the comments of our three Central European trustees. Eda Kriseova singled out the peculiar and precious human intensity of their pre-1989 contacts, as banned writers and underground editors, with these visitors from another world. Gyorgy Bence observed that in his experience CEEPP was one of very few European (as opposed to American) organisations directly involved in supporting dissidents. Jerzy Jedlicki said that on joining the board he had been impressed not only by the expertise we had gathered over the years but also by the total absence of that patronising attitude which so often characterised Western approaches to the supposedly backward benighted denizens of "Eastern Europe".

These memories matter. It matters that intellectuals from the former East know that not everyone in Western Europe lived with their backs to the Berlin Wall. It matters for the future of Europe that even in the history of the continent's East–West division there are fragments, however small, of shared memory.

## *Funders*

*Members of the original consortium:*
Ford Foundation
European Cultural Foundation (*via* European Cooperation Fund)
Rockefeller Brothers Fund
Rockefeller Foundation
Open Society Fund
John D and Catherine T MacArthur Foundation

*Other funders:*
Calouste Gulbenkian Foundation
Conanima Foundation
Fund Praemium Erasmianum
Romanian Legacy (*via* European Cultural Foundation)
Sven Salen Foundation

## *Trustees, Staff and Associates*

# *Catalogue of Activity: Publications, Workshops and Fellowships supported by the Central and East European Publishing Project*

ELIZABETH WINTER

## PUBLICATIONS IN CENTRAL AND EAST EUROPEAN LANGUAGES

### JOURNALS

#### Czech Republic

ACTA: A quarterly journal in Czech and English, published by the Documentation Centre for the Promotion of Independent Czechoslovak Literature, Scheinfeld, Germany, edited by Vilem Precan and Jan Vladislav, with articles and reviews concerning samizdat, literature published in the West and history.

CTENI NA LETO: An almanac containing articles of topical interest and cultural information, published in Rome by Jiri Pelikan, for distribution within Czechoslovakia.

FRANCOUZSKA LITERATURA: Anthologies of modern French literature edited in Paris, in close, clandestine cooperation with translators in Czechoslovakia.

HOST: A literary and cultural journal published in Brno. It concentrates on contemporary Czech literature and poetry, with articles on philosophy, anthropology and literary criticism, focusing on young and less well-known authors. Founded in 1985, it functioned as an underground review for five years and came above ground in 1990.

KRITICKY SBORNIK: Originally a samizdat publication, devoted to a scholarly analysis of literature, and now a legal journal.

LIDOVE NOVINY: Published from 1987 as a samizdat weekly periodical, whose editorial board included Jiri Dienstbier, Petr Pithart, Vaclav Havel, Miroslav Kusy, Zdenek Urbanek among others. They suffered regular harassment under the old regime. Now, after several transformations, one of the leading daily newspapers in the Czech Republic.

LISTY: Founded by Jiri Pelikan in Rome, this bi-monthly publication containing political and cultural articles moved to Prague in 1990.

MOST: The aim of this journal, founded in 1988, was to combine both home and exile Czechoslovak literature. It was published in Germany with contributions from "home" literary figures, most of whom were banned and their work suppressed. The first Editor-in-Chief was Jiri Grusa and the main contact in Czechoslovakia the dramatist Milan Uhde. In 1990, this group formed the basis of the publishing house Atlantis in Brno.

PRI TOMNOST: Initially an underground periodical, with an influential group of editors, including Petr Pithart and Jan Sokol, it has now been revived as a "supplement" to *Literarni noviny*.

PROGLAS: A samizdat periodical based in Brno.

PROSTOR: A socio-cultural journal "of a conservative orientation" published since 1982, originally as an underground publication, by Ales Lederer.

REVOLVER REVUE: A literary journal, published since 1985, originally underground, which has attracted contributions mainly from the younger generation.

150,000 SLOV: An exile anthology, founded in 1981 by Antonin Liehm, dealing with the problems of Central and East Europe. It contained many translated political, historical and philosophical articles for distribution within Czechoslovakia.

STREDNI EVROPA: A political and cultural journal, edited by Rudolf Kucera, originally as an underground publication, with historical and philosophical articles on the problems of Central Europe.

SVET A DIVADLO: A theatrical journal with much translated material.

TVAR: This literary and cultural journal was very influential in the mid-1960s, but ceased to exist after 1968. The editorial board is now compiling a two-volume anthology of selected articles to be published by Stredoevropska nadace.

VOKNO: A quarterly journal with special appeal to young people, focusing on ecology, music, art and film.

VYTVARNE UMENI: A journal of contemporary art, which since 1990 has brought in-depth articles on modern artists to a public previously denied access to such material.

## Hungary

BUKSZ: A review, founded in 1989, with the aim to be a Hungarian counterpart to the *New York Review of Books* or the *Times Literary Supplement*. It combines articles of topical interest with shorter reviews. One of the first book review journals to emerge after the dissolution of the socialist state, it now has an established reputation and faithful readership. The Editor-in-Chief is Gabor Klaniczay.

DOXA: A special issue of this philosophical journal, launched in 1992 as a joint project of Eotvos Lorand University and the Institute of Philosophy of the Hungarian Academy, was published in German with the cooperation of the Viennese journal *Mesotes*.

EGYHAZ ES VILAG: A monthly review launched in 1989 by young liberal intellectuals within and around the Hungarian Reformed Church. It represents a forum for debate for the liberal minorities of all the Christian churches in Hungary.

GOND: A philosophical journal launched in 1991 by the Department of

Philosophy of the Kossuth University in Debrecen, under the general editorship of Professor Mihaly Vajda.

HOLMI: A literary journal, launched in 1989 in Budapest, under the general editorship of Rez Pal. Articles deal with various aspects of aesthetics and criticism.

JELENKOR: A monthly journal, established in 1958 in Pecs, southern Hungary, and highly respected for its coverage of literature and art. It became independent from the state administration in 1989, under the editorship of Istvan Csuhar.

KALLIGRAM: A cultural journal, edited by Lajos Grendel, published in Bratislava for the Hungarian minority in Slovakia.

KATOLIKUS SZEMLE: A Catholic review, first published in Hungary in the 1880s by the Society of St Stephen. After the Communist takeover, it moved to Rome with the chief purpose of restoring the Church's freedom in Hungary. Since 1990, it has become more sporadic, but a special issue devoted to contemporary Polish theology in 1994 received support.

NAPPALI HAZ: A literary quarterly founded in 1989 in Budapest. Considered the most exciting of the many periodicals launched at that time, especially attractive to a younger generation of writers.

## Poland

ACTA POLONIAE HISTORICA: A periodical published by the Institute of History of the Polish Academy of Sciences in several languages, to acquaint foreign scholars with the latest achievements of Polish historiography.

ARKA: A political and cultural journal based in Krakow. It was founded in 1983 under martial law as a samizdat publication to secure a free exchange of ideas and defined its political and philosophical line as neo-liberal or neo-conservative. It became a legal entity in 1990.

BRULION: Originated as an underground literary quarterly in Krakow in 1987 to promote young writers and translations from other East European languages. In 1992, it moved to Warsaw, and became the Brulion Foundation, expanding its activities to publishing volumes of poetry, organising poetry competitions and producing Brulion TV.

KRESY: A literary cultural journal founded in 1989 in Lublin. The special issue to mark its fifth anniversary focused on "neighbours" and "frontiers" with much newly translated material.

KRYTYKA: A journal founded in the late 1970s as an independent underground political quarterly, which quickly earned the reputation of being one of the most influential journals of the Polish opposition. Its editorial board includes Adam Michnik and Jan Kofman.

RES PUBLICA/RES PUBLICA NOWA: Created in 1979 by a group of leading Polish intellectuals as an underground quarterly. It ceased to exist in 1981 under martial law, but reappeared in 1987 as a legal, self-financing and independent monthly. With the arrival of the free-market economy, it faced serious financial problems and, in the end, bankruptcy. In 1992, it re-emerged for the third time as Res Publica Nowa, with a changed, less elitist formula, but still with a serious intellectual profile. Its editor is the highly respected historian and commentator, Marcin Krol.

ZESZYTY LITERACKIE: A quarterly literary magazine, edited by Barbara Torunczyk, founded in Paris in 1983. Originally distributed among Polish emigrés, it also appeared as an underground publication during martial law. It rapidly gained the position of the most important and influential publication of its kind. From 1990, the magazine was printed in Poland and in 1993 the editorial office also moved permanently to Poland. The editorial board remains international (including Peter Kral, Tomas Venclova, Joseph Brodsky) and the magazine cultivates its bridging role between Western and Central European culture.

## Romania

AGORA: A Romanian-language cultural and political journal launched in Pennsylvania by Dorin Tudoran.

CONTRAPUNCT: Launched in Bucharest in 1990 by a group of young Romanian writers, under the general editorship of Hanibal Stanciulescu.

INTERVAL: A cultural journal launched in Brasov in 1990, under the editorship of Gheorghe Craciun.

MANUSCRIPTUM: A periodical devoted to publishing manuscript material to examine the creative literary process, and little-known documents. Until 1990, it received support from the Ministry of Culture and was subject to censorship. It has survived as an annual independent publication, under the editorship of Ruxandra Mihaila.

MEMORIA: The journal of the Memoria Foundation, edited by Banu Radulescu, devoted to the memory of those imprisoned or interned in Romania this century.

SFERA POLITICII: This bi-monthly review has an international editorial board and aims to raise the level of political debate within Romania, and encourage respect for minority groups.

## Slovakia

FILOZOFIA: A special issue of this journal of the Philosophical Faculty of the University of Bratislava was devoted to British philosophy.

FRAGMENT: A literary journal, edited by Oleg Pastier, originally as an underground publication.

## Bulgaria

IZBOR: Monthly magazine of political analysis founded in 1990, edited by Evgenia Ivanova, which works in cooperation with the pan-Central and East European quarterly, *East–East*.

KULTURA: A political and cultural weekly edited by Koprinka Chervenkova, launched in 1990, and held in high esteem by the intellectual elite.

PANORAMA: A quarterly journal founded in 1980. Originally strictly literary, after 1989 it changed its profile to social, political and legal thought.

POLITICAL STUDIES: A quarterly set up in 1991 as an academic publication in the field of political science, edited by Dobrin Kanev.

## Baltic Republics

BALTOS LANKOS: A journal which appears twice yearly in Vilnius, Lithuania. It is an academic journal, aiming at creating a synthesis of various scholarly fields, predominantly hermeneutics, semiotics, and the history and theory of culture. Attached to the Centre for Cultural Studies, one of its main objectives is to unite Lithuanian scholars and their emigré colleagues.

KRANTAI: A cultural monthly, founded in Vilnius in 1988 by the Lithuanian Unions of Theatre and Art, and the Composers' Union. Its readership is not only artists and specialists in cultural affairs, but also the wider public.

SIETYNAS: A Lithuanian cultural review (an "almanac", literally), which started out illegally in 1988, and has since become independent.

VIKERKAAR/RADUGA: A monthly journal which contains a lot of translated material from world literature, founded by the Estonian

Writers' Union in Tallinn in 1988. Its relatively autonomous Russian-language counterpart, *Raduga*, concentrates on liberal ideas and social criticism in Estonia and in the former Soviet Union.

## Croatia

ERASMUS: A bi-monthly journal launched by the Erasmus Guild in 1993 to further the culture of democracy. A high-quality, liberal, independent magazine.

AGORA: A social science journal, launched in a bi-lingual edition in Riyeka in 1994.

## BOOKS

Acton Lord: *Historical, Political and Moral Essays* (in Polish, Res Publica, Warsaw)

Aron R: *Essai sur les libertés* (in Czech, Archa, Bratislava)

Aron R: *Démocratie et totalitarisme* (in Bulgarian, Arges, Sofia)

Babel I: *Diary 1920* (in Czech, Torst, Prague)

Bachelard J: *Le Nouvel Esprit scientifique* (in Serbo-Croat, Izdavacka Z Stojanovica, Novi Sad)

Bachelard J: *La Poétique de la rêverie* (in Bulgarian, Arges, Sofia, 1994)

Baran M: *Sosnowiec jest jak kobieta* (in Polish, Brulion, Warsaw)

Baran M: *The Anonymous Half: An Introduction to Contemporary Feminism* (in Bulgarian, Sansa, Sofia)

Bence G (ed): *Nationalism* (an anthology in Hungarian, Szazadveg, Budapest)

Benevolo L: *The European City* (in Slovak, Archa, Bratislava)

Bergson H: *Les Deux Sources de la morale et de la religion* (in Bulgarian, Arges, Sofia)

Berlin I: *Two Concepts of Liberty* (in Polish, Res Publica, Warsaw)

Besançon A: *Anatomia widma* (in Polish, Res Publica, Warsaw)

Bielecki C: *Z celi do celi* (in Polish, Puls Publications, London)

Blumsztajn S: *Une Pologne hors censure* (in Polish, Association Solidarité France-Pologne, Paris)

Borodziej W: *Od Poczdamu do Szklarskiej Poreby* (in Polish, Aneks, London)

Borsody S: *Monograph* (in Hungarian, Cserepfalvi, Budapest)

Brodsky J: *Spiew Wahadla* (in Polish, Zeszyty Literackie, Paris)

Brodsky J: *82 Wiersze i Poematy* (in Polish, Zeszyty Literackie, Paris)

Brodsky J: *Less Than One* (in Czech, Torst, Prague)

Brown P: *The Cult of the Saints* (in Hungarian, Atlantisz, Budapest)

Burckhardt J: *Kultura Renesanse v Italiji* (Serbo-Croat, Izdavacka Z Stojanovica, Novi Sad)

Burckhardt J: *Die Zeit Konstantins des Grossen* (in Polish, Panstwowy Instytut Wydawniczy, Warsaw)

Burke E: *Reflections on the French Revolution* (in Polish, Res Publica, Warsaw)

Burke E: *Reflections on the French Revolution* (in Hungarian, Atlantisz, Budapest)

Burke E: *Popular Culture in Early Modern Europe* (in Hungarian, Szazdveg, Budapest)

Celan P and Sachs N: *Poetry* (in Polish and German, A5 Wydawnictwo, Poznan)

Cerny V: *Tvorba a osobnost* (in Czech, Odeon, Prague)

Cerny V: *Literary Studies* (in Czech, Mlada Fronta, Prague)

Cerny V: *Essays on European Baroque* (in Czech, Arkyr, Prague)

Chalupecky J (ed): *Na hranicich umeni* (essays by Czech and Slovak artists, in Czech, Arkyr, Rome)

de Chardin P T: *Le Phénomène humain* (in Bulgarian, Arges, Sofia)

Constant B: *The Liberty of the Ancients and the Moderns* (in Hungarian, Atlantisz, Budapest)

Conquest R: *The Harvest of Sorrow* (in Polish, Res Publica, Warsaw)

Crick F: *Istota i pochodzenie zycia* (in Polish, PIW, Warsaw)

Culik J: *Knihy za ohradou* (Trizonia, Prague)

Culler J: *Saussure* (in Slovak, Archa, Bratislava)

Dahrendorf R: *The Modern Social Conflict* (in Slovak, Archa, Bratislava)

Dahrendorf R: *Reflections on the Revolution in Europe* (in Bulgarian, Centre for the Study of Democracy, Sofia)

Dawkins R: *The Blind Watchmaker* (in Polish, PIW, Warsaw)

Deak I: *Beyond Nationalism* (in Hungarian, Gondolat, Budapest)

Dedecek J: *Songs* (in Czech, '68 Publishers, Toronto)

Deleuze G: *A quoi reconnait-on le structuralisme? La Philosophie au XX^e^ siècle* (in Slovak, Archa, Bratislava)

Derrida J: *Texts on Deconstruction* (in Czech, Archa, Bratislava)

Domanski P (ed): *Secret Documents of the Politburo of the Polish Communist Party (PUWP) on the Events of December 1970* (in Polish, Aneks, London)

Doncheva-Petkova et al: *Contributions of Bulgarian Archaeology* (in Bulgarian, Arges, Sofia)

Dudek A and Pytel G: *Piasecki Boleslaw: Proba biografii politycznej* (in Polish, Aneks, London)

Dziewanowski K: *Zlom zelazny, smiech pokoleri* (in Polish, Libella, Paris)

Eco H: *Opera aberta* (in Czech, Torst, Prague)

Eco H: *Europe and the Perfect Language* (in Hungarian, Atlantisz, Budapest)

Eliade M: *Fragments d'un journal* (in Polish, Polonia)

Eliade M: *Samanizm* (in Serbo-Croat, Izdavacka Z Stojanovica, Novi Sad)

Eliade M: *Religia, literatura, i komunizm: Dziennik emigranta* (in Polish, Puls Publications, London)

Feynman R P: *QED: The strange theory of light and matter* (in Polish, PIW, Warsaw)

Fikar L: *Kamen na hrob* (in Czech, Charta 77 Foundation, Stockholm)

Fink E: *Oaza stesi* (in Czech, Mlada Fronta, Prague)

Fiut A: *Moment wieczny: Poezja Czeslawa Milosza* (in Polish, Libella, Paris)

Fol A et al: *A Brief Encyclopedia – Trakijska drevnost* (in Bulgarian, Arges, Sofia)

Friedlander S: *Histoire et psychoanalyse* (in Bulgarian, Arges, Sofia)

Frye N: *The Great Code: The Bible and Literature* (in Hungarian, Budapest)

Garton Ash T: *Mi Gradani 1989* (in Croatian, Novi Liber, Zagreb)

Garton Ash T: *The Germanness of the DDR* (in Polish, Aneks, London)

Garton Ash T: *Stredoevropan volbou* (in Czech, Institut pro stredoevropskou kulturu a politiku, Prague)

Garton Ash T: *We the People* (in Bulgarian, Izbor, Sofia)

Gellner E et al: *Europa i co z tego wynika – Castel Gandolfo Gespräche* (in Polish, Res Publica, Warsaw)

Gellner E: *Nations and Nationalism* (in Hungarian, Tanulmany Kiado, Pecs)

Giddens A: *Sociology* (in Slovak, Archa, Bratislava)

Gombrowicz R: *Gombrowicz w Argentynie: Swiadectwa i dokumenty 1939–1963* (in Polish, Puls Publications, London)

Gombrowicz W: *Diary I* (in Hungarian, Jelenkor, Budapest)

Gombrowicz W: *The Diary* (in Czech, Torst, Prague)

Goodwin et al: *Essays on Anarchism* (in Hungarian, Szazadveg, Budapest)

Gray J: *Liberalism* (in Polish, Res Publica, Warsaw)

Grebenickova R: *The Puzzle of Macha's Journey to Venice* (in Czech, Arkyr, Prague)

Gyurgyak J (ed): *Conservatism* (an anthology in Hungarian, Szazdveg, Budapest)

Habermas J: *The Logic of the Social Sciences* (in Hungarian, Atlantisz, Budapest)

Hankova J: *Letorosty* (in Czech, Charta 77 Foundation, Stockholm)

Havel V: *Asanace* (in Czech, PmD, Munich)

Havel V: *Do ruznych stran: Essays 1983–1989* (in Czech, Documentation Centre, Scheinfeld)

Havel V: *The Power of the Powerless* (in Bulgarian, Izbor, Sofia)

Havlicek A (ed): *Pomfil Series: Philosophy Essays* (in Czech, Institute for Central European Culture and Politics, Prague)

Herder W G: *Selection of Works* (in Czech, Torst, Prague)

Herling-Grudzinski G: *Diary Written at Night 1989–1991* (in Czech, Torst, Prague)

Hobsbawm E: *Nations and Nationalism since 1780: Programme, myth, reality* (in Croatian, Novi Liber, Zagreb)

im Hoff U: *Europe of the Enlightenment* (in Hungarian, Atlantisz, Budapest)

Hoffman E: *Lost in Translation* (in Polish, Aneks, London)

Horakova L: *Hadak – Osud Karikaturisty v Cechach* (in Czech, Mlada Fronta, Prague)

Hrabal B: *Proluky* (in Czech, '68 Publishers, Toronto)

Hrabal B: *Vita nuovo* (in Czech, '68 Publishers, Toronto)

Hrabal B: *Svatby v dome* (in Czech, '68 Publishers, Toronto)

Hume D: *Essays, Vol II* (in Hungarian, Atlantisz, Budapest)

Ivanov T and Ivanov R: *Nicopolis ad Istrum* (in Bulgarian, Arges, Sofia)

Jakobson R: *Poetic Function* (in Czech, H + H Publishers, Prague)

Jaspers K: *Nietzsche: Einführung in das Verständnis seines Philosophierens.* (in Polish, Czytelnik, Warsaw)

Jaspers K: *Filozofija* (in Serbo-Croat, Izdavacka Z Stojanovica, Novi Sad)

Jastrun T: *Fast Zweihundert Jahre schon: Od prawie dwustu lat* (in Polish and German, Veto Verlag, Berlin)

Jastrun T: *W zlotej klatce* (in Polish, Veto Verlag, Berlin)

Jedlicka M: *Essays on Thirty Czech and World Writers* (in Czech, Arkyr, Prague)

Jesenska M: *Selected Writings* (in Czech, Torst, Prague)

Jicinsky Z: *Vznik ceske narodni rady: 1968–69* (in Czech, Index, Cologne)

Julis E: *Blizime se k ohni* (in Czech, Charta 77 Foundation, Stockholm)

Kadlec V: *Dubcek – 1968* (in Czech, Index, Cologne)

Kalista Z: *Velika noc* (in Czech, PmD, Munich)

Kanev D (ed): *Power and Elites: Anthology of Modern Social and Political Thought – Volume I* (in Bulgarian, Political Studies, Sofia)

Kant I: *Deines Lebens Sinn* (in Slovak, Archa, Bratislava)

Kaplan K: *Mocni a bezmocni* (in Czech, '68 Publishers, Toronto)

Karpinski W: *Herb Wygnania* (in Polish, Zeszyty Literackie, Paris)

Kolakowski L: *Cywilizacja na lawie oskarzonych* (in Polish, Res Publica, Warsaw)

Kolakowski L: *Glowne nurty marksizmu* (in Polish, Aneks, London)

Kolakowski L: *Horror Metaphysicus* (in Polish, Res Publica, Warsaw)

Kolakowski L: *Religion: If There is no God, Can the Devil be Saved?* (in Bulgarian, Panorama, Sofia)

Komar M: *Zmeczenie* (in Polish, Libella, Paris)

Konrad G: *Antipolitics* (in Bulgarian, Izbor, Sofia)

Kontler L (ed): *Survivors: Elites and Social Change in History – Selection of articles from international literature* (in Hungarian, Atlantisz, Budapest)

Koskova H: *Hledani ztracene generace* (in Czech, '68 Publishers)

Kotrla I: *Nevitany svedek* (in Czech, Rozrazil, Brno)

Kovacs M: *Liberal Professions and Illiberal Politics* (in Hungarian, Atlantisz, Budapest)

Kovtun G: *The Hilsner Case: T G Masaryk's Fight against Antisemitism* (in Czech, Sefer, Prague)

Krasnodebski Z & Nellen K: *Swiat przezywany* (in Polish, PIW, Warsaw)

Krejci J: *The Civilization of Asia and the Middle East Before the European Challenge* (in Czech, Karolinum, Prague)

Kriseova E: *Arboretum* (in Czech, Arkyr, Rome)

Krol M: *Podroz romantyczna* (in Polish, Libella, Paris)

Krol M: *Slownik Demokracji* (in Polish, Res Publica, Warsaw)

Kucera R: *Komentare* (in Czech, Institut pro stredoevropskou kulturu a politiku, Prague)

Kundera M: *Zycie jest gdzie indziej* (in Polish, Puls Publications, London)

Kuschiev K: *Life in Exile* (in Bulgarian, Arges, Sofia)

Lepkowski T: *Essays* (in Polish, Puls Publications, London)

Levi P: *The Drowned and the Saved* (in Polish, Res Publica, Warsaw)

Lévi-Strauss C: *Myth and Meaning* (in Slovak, Archa, Bratislava)

de Libera A: *La Philosophie médiévale* (in Slovak, Archa, Bratislava)

Lotman J M: *Text and Culture* (in Slovak, Archa, Bratislava)

Ludassy M (ed): *Anglo-American Liberalism* (an anthology in Hungarian, Atlantisz, Budapest)

Macfarlane A: *The Origins of English Individualism* (in Hungarian, Szazadveg, Budapest)

Maj B: *Zaglada swietego miasta* (in Polish, Puls Publications, London)

Malcolm N: *Ludwig Wittgenstein – A Memoir* (in Slovak, Archa, Bratislava)

Malewski J: *Ptasznik z Wilna: O Jozefie Mackiewiczu* (in Polish, Arka, Krakow)

Manent P: *Histoire intéllectuelle du libéralisme* (in Hungarian, Tanulmany Kiado, Pecs)

Mannheim K: *Ideology and Utopia* (in Czech, Archa, Bratislava)

Maruste R (ed): *Human Rights and the Administration of Justice* (in Estonian, Faatum, Tallinn)

Merrill J: *Wybor Poezjii* (in Polish, Zeszyty Literackie, Paris)

Mestan A: *Ceska Literatura 1785–1985* (in Czech, '68 Publishers, Toronto)

Michnik A: *Essays* (in Hungarian, Magyar Fuzetek, Paris)

Michnik A: *The Devil of Today* (in Bulgarian, Izbor, Sofia)

Michnik A: *The Power of Taste* (in Hungarian, Tanulmany Kiado, Pecs)

Milosz C: *Zotroceny duch* (in Czech, Torst, Prague)

Miroiu A: *Existence of God* (in Romanian, Sansa, Bucharest)

Mlynar Z: *Praga 1968* (in Hungarian, Magyar Fuzetek, Paris)

Mollat du Jourdin M: *Europe and the Sea* (in Slovak, Archa, Bratislava)

Mollat du Jourdin M: *Europe and the Sea* (in Hungarian, Atlantisz, Budapest)

Monikova L: *The Facade* (in Czech, '68 Publishers, Toronto)

Montanari M: *History and the Culture of Food* (in Slovak, Archa, Bratislava)

Montanari M: *History of Food and Alimentation in Europe* (in Hungarian, Atlantisz, Budapest)

*"My tu zyjemy jak w obozie warownym." Listy PPS-WRN Warszawa – Londyn 1940–1945* (in Polish, Puls Publications, London)

Nadeau M: *Histoire du Surréalisme* (in Bulgarian, Arges, Sofia)

Nellen K and Krasnodebski Z (eds): *Lebenswelt* (in Polish, Res Publica, Warsaw)

Novak J: *Prague in Velvet* (in Czech, '68 Publishers, Toronto)

Oakeshott M: *Rationalism and Other Essays* (in Polish, Res Publica, Warsaw)

Olivova V (ed): *Papers of Amelia Posse* (in Czech, H + H Publishers, Prague)

Opat J: *Filozof a politik TGM 1882–1883* (in Czech, Index, Cologne)

Oravcova M (ed): *Philosophy of Natural Language: Collection of Essays* (in Slovak, Archa, Bratislava)

Orwell G: *Collected Essays* (in Czech, Atlantis, Brno)

Ourednik P: *Smirbuch Jazyka Ceskeho* (in Czech, Edice K, Prague)

Paine T et al: *Az angolszasz liberalizmus klasszikusai I.* (in Hungarian, Atlantisz, Budapest)

Patocka J: *Collected works* (in Czech, samizdat, Prague)

Pavel T G: *The Feud of Language* (in Romanian, Univers, Bucharest)

Pawlak A: *Trudny wybor wierszy: Schwierige Gedicht-Auswahl.* (Poems) (in Polish, Veto Verlag, Berlin)

Pekarkova I: *Pera a perute* (in Czech, '68 Publishers, Toronto)

Piaget J: *La Psychologie de l'enfant* (in Serbo-Croat, Izdavacka Z Stojanovica, Novi Sad)

Pilinszky J: *Selected Poems and Essays* (in Czech, Torst, Prague)

Pipes R: *The Russian Revolution* (in Polish, PWN, Warsaw)

Pithart P et al: *The Czechs in Modern Times* (in Czech, Rozmluvy, Prague)

Pithart P: *Osmasedesaty* (in Czech, Rozmluvy, Surrey)

Plackov I P: *Memories and Reminiscences* (in Bulgarian, Arges)

Podsiadlo J: *Wiersze wybrane (Poems)* (in Polish, Brulion, Warsaw)

*Polska 5 lat po sierpniu. Raport* (in Polish, Aneks, London)

Polkowski J: *Wiersze (1977–1984)* (in Polish, Puls Publications, London)

Prochazkova L: A *Co si o tom myslite vy?* (in Czech, Charta 77 Foundation, Stockholm)

Prochazkova L: *Smolna kniha* (in Czech, '68 Publishers, Toronto)

Putna M C: *Russia Outside Russia* (in Czech, Petrov Publishing House, Brno)

Rehnicer R: *L'Herbe et les Elephants: Reflexions sur l'environment humain au cours d'une guerre civile* (in Czech, Prostor, Prague)

Reich R B: *The Work of Nations* (in Czech, Prostor, Prague)

Richterova S: *ABC-Book of the Father's Tongue* (in Czech, Arkyr-Rome/Atlantis-Brno)

Richterova S: *Slova a Ticho* (in Czech, Arkyr, Rome)

Ricoeur P: *Temps et recit* (in Serbo-Croat, Izdavacka Z Stojanovica, Novi Sad)

Ricoeur P: *Histoire et vérité* (in Bulgarian, Arges, Sofia)

Rupnik J: *The Other Europe* (in Czech, Prostor, Prague)

Russell B: *Selected Writings* (in Czech, Svoboda, Prague)

Russell B: *Theory of Knowledge* (in Bulgarian, Critique and Humanism, Sofia)

Rutkowski K: *Braterstwo albo smierc: Zabijanie Mickiewicza w Kole Bozym* (in Polish, Libella, Paris)

Sartori G: *The Theory of Democracy Revisited* (in Bulgarian, Centre for the Study of Democracy, Sofia)

Scruton R: *A History of Philosophy* (in Bulgarian, Panorama, Sofia)

Sendecki M: Z *wysokosci. Wiersze z lat 1985–90. (Poems)* (in Polish, Brulion, Warsaw)

Shakespeare W: *Romeo and Juliet, Hamlet, Julius Caesar, Richard II, Henry IV (Parts 1 and 2), Richard II* (translated by Zdenek Urbanek into Czech, Atlantis/Most, Brno)

Shalamov V: *The Kolyma Stories* (in Czech, Mlada Fronta, Prague)

Shklar J: *Montesquieu* (in Hungarian, Atlantisz, Budapest)

Spilarova O: *An Anthology of French Literature* (in Czech, Paris, 1988)

Stanosz B (ed): *Philosophy of Language* (in Polish, Spacja, Warsaw)

Starobinski J: *Kriticki Odnos* (in Serbo–Croat, Izdavacka Z Stojanovica, Novi Sad, 1990)

Starobinski J: *L'Invention de la liberté* (in Polish, Czytelnik, Warsaw)

Stern J P: *The Heart of Europe* (in Czech, Torst, Prague)

Stone N: *Europe Transformed* (in Polish, Res Publica, Warsaw)

Strauss L: *Persecution and the Art of Writing* (in Hungarian, Atlantisz, Budapest)

Suchecki J: *Przygody Protago* (in Polish, Brulion, Warsaw)

Swietlicki M: *Zimne Kraje: Wiersze 1980–1990.* (Poems) (in Polish, Brulion, Warsaw)

Synek M: *Nadeje a zklamani: Prazske jaro 1968* (in Czech, Documentation Centre, Scheinfeld)

Szaruga L: *Nie mowcie Europa. Sagt nicht Europa* (Poems) (in Polish, Poglad, Berlin)

Talmon J L: *The Origins of Totalitarian Democracy* (in Czech, Slon, Prague)

Tatarka D: *Listy do Vecnosti* (in Slovak, '68 Publishers, Toronto)

Tennant P (ed): *Correspondence of A Posse-Brazdova* (in Czech, Benes Institute, Prague)

de Tocqueville A: *L'Ancien Régime* (in Hungarian, Atlantisz, Budapest)

Trznadel J: *Polski Hamlet: Klopoty z dzialaniem* (in Polish, Libella, Paris)

Tuck R: *Hobbes* (in Hungarian, Atlantisz, Budapest)

Urbanek Z: *Essays* (in Czech, Arkyr, Rome)

Urbanek Z: *Actors Build the Space* (in Czech, Arkyr, Prague)

Uspienski B A and Zywow W M: *Car i bog* (in Polish, PIW, Warsaw)

Vaculik L: *Mili spoluzaci* (in Czech, Index, Cologne)

Venclova T: *Rozmowa w Zimie* (in Polish, Zeszyty Literackie, Paris)

Vincenz S: *Tajak – tortenclemmel* (in Hungarian, Jelenkor, Pecs)

Vrkocova L: *Music in Ghetto Terezin* (in Czech, Arkyr, Rome)

Wagner R: *The Dusk of Myths* (in Bulgarian, Izbor, Sofia)

Walicki A: *Trzy Patriotyzmy* (in Polish, Res Publica)

Weber M: *Wirtschaft und Gesellschaft* (in Hungarian, Kozgazdasagi Jogi Konyvkiado)

Wellek R & Warren A: *Theory of Literature* (in Czech, Odeon, Prague)

Welsch W: *Aesthetisches Denken* (in Slovak, Archa, Bratislava)

Wernisch I: *Zil Nebel* (in Czech, PmD, Munich)

Wilkins W J: *Hindu Mythology* (in Bulgarian, Arges, Sofia)

Wittgenstein L: *Tractatus Logico-philosophicus* (in Czech, Svoboda, Prague)

Wittgenstein L: *Vermischte Bemerkungen* (in Hungarian, Atlantisz, Budapest)

Wittgenstein L: *Vermischte Bemerkungen* (in Czech, Mlada Fronta, Prague)

*Yearbook on Polish Studies in Human Rights* (in Polish, Poznan Human Rights Committee)

Zagajewski A: *Solidarnosc i samotnosc* (in Polish, Zeszyty Literackie, Paris)

Zagajewski A: *Plotno* (in Polish, Zeszyty Literackie, Paris)

Zagajewski A: *Dwa miasta* (in Polish, Zeszyty Literackie, Paris)

Zaleski M: *Madvemu biada? Szkice Literackie* (in Polish, Libella, Paris)

Znepolski I (ed): *Mass Communications and Society: Anthology of Modern Social and Political Thought – Volume II* (in Bulgarian, Political Studies, Sofia)

## OCCASIONAL PUBLICATIONS

**Archa (Bratislava):**
Pocket Philosophy Series (1994)

**Documentation Centre (Scheinfeld):**
*Demokraticka revoluce – Stav a vyhledy sveta, Jaro 1989* (in Czech, 1988)

**Institute of Contemporary History (Prague):**
*Czechoslovakia and the Marshall plan – Selected documents* (in Czech, 1992)
*Metamorphosis of the Prague Spring 1968–1969; Selected studies and documents* (in Czech, 1993)
*H Gordon Skilling: 1912–1992* (publication on the occasion of his 80th birthday, in Czech, 1992)

**Centre for Research into Communist Economies (London):**
*Sirc Jlubo: Sta da se radi sa privredom?* (in Serbo-Croat, 1988)

**Kultura (Paris):**
*Kultura i jej krag 1946–1986* (catalogue of the exhibition in December 1986 – January 1987, in Polish)
*Protokoly tzw. Komisji Grabskiego: Dokumenty* (in Polish, 1986)

**Institute for Central European Culture and Politics (Prague):**
*Pomfil: Study texts in sociology, philosophy and political science* (in Czech, 1991–1994)

**Res Publica (Warsaw):**
*O kryzysie – Castel Gandolfo Gespräche* (in Polish, 1990)

**SLON (Prague):**
*Social and cultural anthropology* (in Czech, 1993)

**Arkyr (Rome):**
*Generace 35–45, sbornik* (in Czech, 1986)

**Michael Polanyi Liberal Philosophical Association (Budapest):**
*Polanyiana* (in Hungarian, 1992)

**The Museum of Czech Literature (Prague):**
Video cassettes of Czech writers and scholars (to be used for schools)

# PUBLICATIONS IN WESTERN LANGUAGES

## JOURNALS

### English

BUDAPEST REVIEW OF BOOKS: A quarterly launched in 1991. Articles from the parent journal, BUKSZ, are translated for an international audience. Subscribers include many American and British university libraries.

CROSS CURRENTS: A yearbook of Central European culture, edited by Ladislav Matejka. It first appeared in 1982 from Ann Arbor, Michigan, and is now published by Yale University Press. It features fiction, poetry, debate and art in reproduction, and has been instrumental in furthering the debate about Central Europe and culture in the region.

EAST EUROPEAN REPORTER: A quarterly launched in 1985, containing news and articles about human rights issues in Eastern Europe, with contributions from within these countries. A forum for exchanging information between the countries of the Eastern bloc and a source of information for Western journalists and academics.

FROM THE LOGICAL POINT OF VIEW: A philosophical journal published in Prague, edited by Dr Antonin Kosik of the Institute of Philosophy.

INTERNATIONAL JOURNAL OF ROMANIAN STUDIES: This learned journal was published in Amsterdam as a forum for independent scholarship and academic debate, at a time when all study in Romania was subject to rigorous censorship.

HELSINKI MONITOR: In 1994, a special issue of this journal was devoted to a debate between writers from Belgrade and Zagreb, in an attempt to encourage fruitful discussion in the war-torn countries.

SOCIAL RESEARCH: This well-established journal of the New School for Social Research, New York, under the editorship of Arien Mack, has devoted four thematic issues to Central and Eastern Europe, with many contributions from scholars in the region.

TRAFIKA: A literary journal based in Prague, which aims to make outstanding works of fiction and poetry available to the widest possible readership.

## French

L'AUTRE EUROPE: The focus of this journal, published in Paris, is debate of relevance to Central Europe. It includes a great deal of translated material.

LES CAHIERS DE L'EST: The Romanian writer and editor, Dumitru Tsepeneag, re-launched this literary journal in Paris in 1990, focusing mainly on contemporary writing, fiction and poetry.

LES CAHIERS DE PHILOSOPHIE: A special issue of this learned journal was devoted to the Czech philosopher, Jan Patocka, including much newly translated material.

LETTRE INTERNATIONAL: This bi-monthly literary and cultural journal, originally in French and published in Paris, brought much original writing from Eastern Europe to the attention of a wide readership, under the editorship of Antonin Liehm. There are now many different editions throughout Europe, with independent editorial boards which work closely together.

## German

TRANSIT: A scholarly and cultural journal, edited by the Institute for Human Sciences, Vienna, and published by Neue Kritik, Frankfurt. It deals thematically with various social, political and historical topics of relevance to Central Europe, aiming to bring these debates to the attention of readers in Germany and Austria.

## Portuguese

APPROXIMAÇOES: A cultural journal edited by Henryk Siewerski and published in Brazil, bringing translated material from Eastern Europe to the intellectual community in South America.

## BOOKS

Alexandrescu S (ed): *Roemenie – Verhalen van deze tijd* (an anthology of short stories, translated into Dutch from the Romanian, Meulenhoff)

Andric I: *The Days of the Consuls* (translated from Serbo-Croat into English, Forest Books, London)

Beksiak J et al: *The Polish Transformation: Programme and Progress* (Centre for Research into Communist Economies, London)

Bialostocki J et al: *Castelgandolfo-Gespräche 1985: Über die Krise* (Institut für die Wissenschaften vom Menschen, Vienna)

Bibo I: *Democracy, Revolution, Self-Determination* (translated into English from the Hungarian, Atlantic Research & Publication, New Jersey)

Blandiana A: *The Hour of Sand* (selected poems, translated into English from the Romanian, Anvil Press Poetry, London)

Böckenförde E W et al: *Castelgandolfo-Gespräche 1985: Der Mensch in den modernen Wissenschaften* (IWM, Vienna)

Bodor A (ed): *Hongarije – Verhalen van deze tijd* (an anthology of short stories, translated into Dutch from the Hungarian, Meulenhoff)

Bozoki A et al (eds): *Post-communist Transition: Emerging pluralism in Hungary* (Pinter Publishers, London)

Capek K: *Plays* (translated into French from the Czech, Editions de l'Aube, France)

Czerniawski A (ed): *The Mature Laurel* (essays on modern Polish poetry, translated into English from the Polish, Seren Books, Wales)

Dery T: *Giant Baby* (translated into English from the Hungarian, Theatre Studies Publications, Glasgow University)

Detrez R (ed): *Bulgarije – Verhalen van deze tijd* (an anthology of short stories, translated into Dutch from the Bulgarian, Meulenhoff)

Dumitrascu A et al: *Young Poets of a New Romania* (translated into English from the Romanian, Forest Books, London)

Eekman T (ed): *Joegoslavie – Verhalen van deze tijd* (an anthology of short stories, translated into Dutch from the Serbo-Croat, Meulenhoff)

Goetz-Stankiewicz M (ed) *Goodbye Samizdat! An anthology of samizdat writings* (translated into English from the Czech and Slovak, Northwestern University Press, Illinois)

Goma P: *My Childhood at the Gate of Unrest* (translated into English from the Romanian, Readers International, London)

Hamvas B: *Essays* and *Karneval* (translated into French from the Hungarian, Editions l'Age d'Homme, Switzerland)

Hankiss A: *A Hungarian Romance* (translated from Hungarian into English, Readers International, London)

Hankiss E: *Hongrie diagnostiques: essai en pathologie sociale* (translated into French from the Hungarian, Georg Editeur, Geneva)

Havel V: *Political Essays* (translated into French from the Czech, Editions Calmann-Levy, Paris)

Havel V: *The Anatomy of Reticence: Eastern European Dissidents and the Peace Movement in the West* (translated into English from the Czech, Charta 77 Foundation, Stockholm)

Havel V: *Politics and Conscience* (translated into English from the Czech, Charta 77 Foundation, Stockholm)

Havel V: *About Theatre – texts from the samizdat periodical of the same name* (translated into English from the Czech, Charta 77 Foundation, Stockholm)

Kaplan K: *Report on the Murder of the General Secretary – The Slansky Trials* (translated into English from the Czech, Ohio State University Press)

Kersten K: *The Establishment of Communist Rule in Poland 1943–48* (translated into English from the Polish, University of California Press)

Kertesz I: *Kaddisch für ein nicht geborenes Kind* (in German, Rowohlt Verlag, Berlin)

Kis J: *Politics in Hungary: For a Democratic Alternative* (Atlantic Research & Publications, New Jersey)

Klima I: *Judge on Trial* (translated into English from the Czech, Chatto & Windus, London)

Klima I: *Le Grand Roman* (translated into French from the Czech, La Difference, Paris)

Klima L: *Postmortalien* (translated into German from Czech, Sirene, Paris)

Kostrzewa R: *Writings from Kultura: Between East and West* (translated into English from the Polish, Hill & Wang)

Kosztolanyi Dezso: *Skylark* (translated into English from Hungarian, Chatto & Windus, London)

Kozlowski M: *The Polish–Ukrainian Conflict 1918–1919: The Forgotten War* (translated into English from the Polish, Peter Lang Publishing Inc., New York)

Lengyel P: *Cobblestone* (translated from Hungarian into English, Readers International, London)

Lesman K (ed): *Polen – Verhalen van deze tijd* (an anthology of short stories translated into Dutch from the Polish, Meulenhoff)

Lomax W: *Hungarian Workers' Councils in 1956* (translated into English from the Hungarian, Atlantic Research & Publications, New Jersey)

Malowist M: *Modern Economic History in Poland* (in English, University of Geneva Press, Geneva)

Manea N: *Het verhoor* (translated into Dutch from the Romanian, Meulenhoff, Amsterdam)

Michnik A: *The Church and the Left* (translated from Polish into English, University of Chicago Press, Chicago)

Morawski S: *Postmodernity* (translated from Polish into English, Routledge, London)

Nadas P: *The Book of Memories* (translated into Dutch from the Hungarian, Van Gennep, Amsterdam)

Neruda J: *Prague Tales* (translated into English from the Czech, Chatto & Windus, London)

Oprescu D: *East European Democracy without Variable Geometry: The Romanian Case* (translated into English from the Romanian)

Patocka J: *L'Idée de l'Europe en Bohème* (translated into French from the Czech, Editions Jerome Millon, Paris)

Petri G: *Nightsong of the Personal Shadow* (translated into English from the Hungarian, Bloodaxe Books, Newcastle)

Raicu L: *Gogol, Le Fantastique de la banalité* (translated into French from the Romanian, Editions l'Age d'Homme, Switzerland)

Schöpflin G, Wood N et al: *In Search of Central Europe* (Polity Press, Cambridge)

Schuller A: *Does Market Socialism Work?* (Centre for Research into Communist Economies, London)

Skilling Gordon H: *Civic Freedom in Central Europe* (Macmillan Press, London)

Spiro G: *Les Anonymes* (translated into French from the Hungarian, Bernard Coutaz, Paris)

Spiro G et al: *Contemporary Drama: Hungary* (translated into English from the Hungarian, PAJ Publications, New York)

Staniszkis J: *The Ontology of Socialism* (translated into English from the Polish, Oxford University Press, Oxford)

Suto A et al: *Drama Contemporary: Hungary* (translated into English from Hungarian, PAJ Publications, New York)

Szacki J: *Liberalism after Communism* (translated from Polish, Central European University Press, Budapest)

Tamas G M: *The Tribes of Europe* (translated into English from the Hungarian, Institute of Philosophy, Budapest)

Tischner J: *Das Menschliche Drama* (translated into German from the Polish, Wilhelm Fink Verlag)

Vaculik L: *A Cup of Coffee with my Interrogator* (translated from Czech into English, Readers International, London)

Vaculik L: *The Czech Dreambook* (translated from Czech into English, Random House, New York)

Vajda M: *Der postmoderne Heidegger* (in German, Passagen Verlag, Berlin)

*Young Poets of a New Romania* (translated into English from the Romanian, Forest Books, London)

## OCCASIONAL PUBLICATIONS

**Centre for Research into Communist Economies (London):**

*Poland: Stagnation, Collapse or Growth?* (a report by an independent group of economists in Poland, 1988)

**Charta 77 Foundation (Stockholm)**

*Om Tjernobyl, ekonomi, ungdormsproblemsvran* (1986)

*Charta 77 tio ar* (1987)

*Ingen 'jazznost' i Prag* (1987)

*'Foltes tidning' kommen ut igen* (1989)

*Den 'leende revolutionens ritter'* (1990)

*Antligen!* (1990)

(all in Swedish)

*Humour and Silent Screams; Five Czechoslovakian artists in exile on the occasion of the 10th anniversary of Charter 77* (1987)

**Documentation Centre (Scheinfeld):**

*Ten Years of Charter 77* (1986)

*T G Masaryk and our Times* (1986)

*Democracy for all: Manifesto of the movement for Civic Liberties* (1988)

**New Beginnings (Glasgow):**

*Points East Conference Data* (papers from a conference on East European arts, 1991)

**Pubwatch (New York):**

*Directory of Western Organisations Assisting Book Culture in Central and Eastern Europe and the former Soviet Union* (an updated version, jointly with CEEPP, 1994)

# WORKSHOP ON PUBLISHING IN CENTRAL AND EASTERN EUROPE, NOVEMBER 1991

A one-day workshop on "Publishing in Central and Eastern Europe: How can we help?" was held at St Antony's College, Oxford, on 7 November 1991.

## AIMS

The main aim of this workshop was to hear from publishers from Eastern Europe about the problems they were facing in maintaining high standards of book production under the new conditions. Publishers from Western Europe shared their experience of publishing in "free-market" conditions, and representatives of government institutions, foundations, training agencies and other specialists spoke of existing assistance schemes and plans for the future.

## ORGANISATION

The workshop was chaired by Ralf Dahrendorf (Warden of St Antony's College and Chairman of the Central and East European Publishing Project) and sponsored jointly by CEEPP and the British Publishers Association, with additional assistance from the British Council.

## STRUCTURE

### The view from Central and Eastern Europe

Publishers from Slovakia, Romania, Bulgaria, Poland and Hungary presented papers on the current situation in their countries. While the need to differentiate between the "ex-communist" countries was clear, the problems described were broadly similar. The following were among the main points raised:

- The need to "educate governments" about the specific characteristics of the book trade as opposed to other spheres of economic activity; hence the need in each country to develop effective lobbying associations of publishers and booksellers;
- The need for technical assistance in the use of computers, in accountancy and stock-keeping, in desk-top publishing, etc., and the need for management re-training;
- The under-capitalization especially of private publishing, and the lack of access to credit for investment in modern equipment; hence the need for direct financial assistance or investment through joint ventures;
- The problem of payment for foreign rights, especially where these had been contracted to sub-agents;
- The need for both financial and editorial help in particular book projects: e.g. anthologies of Western writings or other translations;
- The need for greater cooperation between publishers, many of whom shared similar problems and could effectively pool ideas;
- The need for more systematic information about the book trades in each country (e.g. for the equivalent of publications such as *Who's Who in Publishing* or *The Bookseller*, as well as regular book reviews);
- The overwhelming problem of distribution since the collapse of the state distributors: this was the single most pressing problem identified by all the speakers;
- The need to support the demand rather than the supply side of the book trade: i.e. to build up libraries and subsidise readers, especially students, so that publishers could charge a realistic price for their books. This point was eloquently endorsed by Sir Roger Elliott, Chairman of the Oxford University Press, who emphasised that academic publishing in Britain could not exist without such indirect subsidies.

## Western proposals and initiatives

Reports were heard from the Publishers Association, the London-based Book House Training Centre, the New York-based organisation Pubwatch, the British Council, the Joint Assistance Unit of the British Foreign Office (known as the Know-How Fund) and the Ausstellungs- und Messe-GmbH des Börsenverein des Deutschen Buchhandels, as well as from Timothy Rix, ex-chairman of the Longman Group; Jessica Douglas-Home, Director of the Eminescu Trust; Csaba Lengyel de Bagota of the British Executive Service Overseas; and Anthony Read, Managing Director of International Book Development.

The variety of levels at which initiatives were being carried out was striking. At the "macro" level, the World Bank and the British Know-How Fund were sponsoring comprehensive studies of the book sector in the various Central and East European countries, on the basis of which recommendations for large-scale programmes of assistance have been or will be made. At the opposite end of the spectrum are a number of small foundations – of which CEEPP may be regarded as one – which concentrate on small-scale direct help to publishers and booksellers.

Whereas Anthony Read, whose organisation was carrying out the World Bank sector studies, emphasised the size of the problems involved and the need to effect wholesale change through influencing government policy, Jessica Douglas-Home of the Eminescu Trust stressed the usefulness of what one participant described as "partisan activities", such as the purchase of a single vehicle which would at least temporarily solve the distribution problems of one independent publisher.

Between these extremes lay a range of initiatives, including:

- book presentation programmes, especially in the sphere of English Language Teaching, business, management, and economics, organised and funded by the British Council and the Know-How Fund; and support for translation in these spheres;

- the "consciousness-raising" and "networking" efforts of the Publishers Association's East European Task Force and of Pubwatch, which have effectively mobilised both funding agencies and individual publishers and, in both cases, organised a series of useful East–West seminars and training workshops;
- The sophisticated re-training programmes for top publishing and bookselling executives, organised by the Book House Training Centre, the German Börsenverein, and others;
- The provision by the British Executive Service Overseas of specialist consultants in publishing (usually retired executives) who at minimal cost can assist, e.g. in the restructuring of state publishing houses;
- The organisation in several countries of "internships" in Western publishing houses for Eastern European publishing executives.

## Information and contacts

The exchange of information summarised above occupied most of the day, and it was generally agreed that this exercise in itself was extremely useful. While all of those present were acquainted with at least some of the other participants, this had been a uniquely comprehensive gathering of those involved in assisting or developing publishing in Central and Eastern Europe.

A number of speakers stressed the need for more regular and systematic contacts, both among Western institutions involved in various forms of assistance, and among publishers in the different countries of Central and Eastern Europe. There were several suggestions for effecting this, including:

- institutionalising meetings such as the present workshop;
- setting up a newsletter on current Western initiatives;
- publishing a guide to agencies or institutions offering help;
- providing training workshops for Central and Eastern European publishers on a thematic rather than a national basis, to bring together publishers from more than one country in the region;

- organising smaller meetings or "mini book fairs" on specific themes for publishers from both East and West, with the aim of exchanging information on book projects and developing ideas for joint publications.

## CONCLUSIONS AND RECOMMENDATIONS

Ralf Dahrendorf suggested that two related sets of questions had been broached at this Workshop, which could be summarised under the following headings: first, *Whom to Help?* – should financial and other support be directed to publishers, distributors, or the "demand" side of the book trade? Second, *How to Help?* – aside from financial aid, was training, information or "networking" the priority?

### *Whom to help?*

There seemed to be general agreement, as suggested above, that while there was still a need at present for some direct help to publishers (whether in the form of support for individual titles, the purchase of equipment, or help in obtaining foreign rights – possibly with the assistance of a "rights clearing house"), "normality" in the book trade could be achieved in the long term only by (a) solving the distribution problem; (b) shifting support from the supply to the demand side.

On the question of distribution, several specific proposals were made, including the need to develop the equivalent in each country of *Books in Print* and the introduction of the Bar Code, and some general points: for example, that the distribution of books did not substantially differ from the distribution of other kinds of goods, and that lessons in this respect might usefully be learned from other sectors of the economy.

### *How to help?*

As indicated above, the need to develop all three areas of assistance – training, information and networking – was endorsed. On the question of training, Euan Henderson of the Book House Training Centre stressed that an important goal of any training scheme should be to ensure that the process of training would continue and develop once the initial scheme was over, i.e. that publishers and booksellers within each country would develop the capacity to undertake such training themselves. The need for more cohesion and a sensible "division of labour" among the various training agencies – British, American, German and French – was also mentioned.

Though one speaker questioned the value of "internships" for Central and East European publishers in Western publishing houses, others argued that this provided a useful experience for publishing executives. Frances Pinter of the Publishers Association's East European Task Force mentioned that some thirty British publishers had expressed willingness to participate in an internship scheme, and Sally Laird suggested that CEEPP might be able to assist in administering such a scheme, if appropriate funding could be found.

In conclusion, Ralf Dahrendorf remarked that the workshop had rightly focused on practical problems and proposals, rather than on more abstract questions, although it was important, in the midst of practicalities, to remember why the freedom and ability to publish books and journals mattered so greatly in the present situation in Central and Eastern Europe.

# WORKSHOP ON THE FUTURE OF JOURNALS IN CENTRAL AND EASTERN EUROPE, JANUARY 1993

A workshop was held on "The Future of Journals in Central and Eastern Europe" at St Antony's College, Oxford, on 15–16 January 1993:

## AIMS

The main aim of the workshop was to bring together editors of journals from East and West Europe, to exchange views and experience and to explore strategies for survival.

## ORGANISATION

The workshop was organised by CEEPP and co-hosted by the *Times Literary Supplement* (TLS). Additional sponsorship was provided by the Conanima Foundation and the Soros Foundations. It was attended by well over one hundred editors (including more than fifty editors of Central and East European journals), specialists on the region and representatives of concerned institutions.

## STRUCTURE

### The journal in the West

The first morning was devoted to presentations from editors of a range of West European journals. Opening the conference, Ralf Dahrendorf drew on his experience both of today's Europe and of post-war Germany to stress the importance of journals as points of connection – connecting people both within countries and across borders, and helping to counter the "dangerous cosiness of small homogeneous tribal units".

Ferdinand Mount, Editor of the TLS, chaired the first session, and indicated in his presentation some of the strategies for survival open to cultural journals, such as advertising, sales, the support of a large magnate, private or public subsidy, while emphasising the need for effective cost control, especially at moments of expansion or investment in more sophisticated technology. Bill Webb, long-time Literary Editor of the *Guardian*, then reflected on some of the differences between the literary and journalistic cultures of East and West, in particular the moral and intellectual role played by the so-called "thick" journals in Russia, and questioned whether this tradition should be allowed to whither away through the "logic" of the market. Antonia Byatt, Literary Officer of the Arts Council of Great Britain, spoke about the ways in which public funding – provided by government, but administered independently – was distributed in Britain to support commercially non-viable journals, which nevertheless played an important cultural role. While arguing that such support was necessary, she outlined some of the problems involved, such as the questionable desirability of keeping small magazines on a "drip-feed", enabling them to survive but never expand. Michael Schmidt of *PN Review*, Paul Barker of *New Society*, Tim Adams of *Granta* and Tilman Spengler of *Kursbuch* then gave brief case histories of their journals. Several themes emerged: editorial commitment as the *sine qua non* of "success"; the "unorthodoxy" of small magazines, and their role in expanding the boundaries of debate; the need for a flexible approach to marketing and fund-raising; the threat from an increasingly "televisual" culture and from the changing role of newspapers, with their increased coverage of arts and cultural life in general.

## The journal in Central and Eastern Europe

In the afternoon, editors from East European countries presented their journals and spoke of the new problems and opportunities arising from the collapse of the old structures. In his introductory remarks to the second session, Timothy Garton Ash outlined the main areas of concern for journals in Central and Eastern Europe. In particular, he posed the question of whether it was inevitable that the free market would kill off the very journals which had once advocated the free market, and whether "dissent" or "dissidence" were part of the self-understanding of journals.

Presentations were given by representatives of a wide variety of journals: Koprinka Chervenkova spoke of the Bulgarian weekly *Kultura*, which aims to bring a note of questioning and doubt to the strident, polarised debate about "good" and "bad" democracy in Bulgaria; Martin Hala spoke of the evolution of the Czech journal *Revolver Revue*, which had started out as an underground journal and was now moving away from its original "social function" to focus on purely cultural issues; Gabor Klaniczay of the *Budapest Review of Books (BUKSZ)* spoke of the need for a new style of critical writing which this journal was trying to promote; Henryk Wozniakowski reviewed the long history of the Krakow-based Catholic journal *Znak*, reflecting on the difficulties of transition in Poland from the "heroic period" of the opposition journals from the late 1970s, and the need to adopt a more sophisticated theoretical approach; Gheorghe Craciun of the Transylvanian journal *Interval* spoke of the difficulties literary magazines experienced in Romania following the withdrawal of support from the Writers' Union and the need to diversify in the attempt to become self-supporting; Saulius Zukas of the scholarly Lithuanian journal *Baltos Lankos* spoke of the desire to move away from past internal conflict "towards Europe". The exchange of views in the following wide-ranging discussion threw up three main themes: the desirability for more international cooperation between editorial staff; the problem of reaching potential readers, i.e. distribution; and the question of direct subsidy and accountability.

## Strategies in the 1990s

The third session was addressed by representatives of several foundations, with a view to finding practical solutions to the problems discussed. Dr J H Meerdink of the Prins Bernhard Fonds, the Netherlands, suggested that perhaps it was time for a more cooperative approach with journals pooling limited resources and coordinating applications for financial support. Mr George Soros outlined the activities of the network of Soros Foundations in the region, many of which were represented. At a time of transition, when purchasing power had collapsed, there was clearly a case for external support. He also expressed an interest in the question of funding reduced subscriptions for libraries and educational institutions. After further discussion, three working groups were formed to examine the practicalities in further detail.

## CONCLUSIONS AND RECOMMENDATIONS

### International cooperation

The desire expressed for access to knowledge of what was being written elsewhere in Europe should be followed up by a pilot project to compile an "Abstract of Journals", with contributions in English from editorial staff, for distribution to all contributors. CEEPP undertook to investigate this further.

### Distribution

Laurens van Krevelen stressed the importance here of cooperation between editors in, for instance, sharing subscriber lists. Editors could also be more active in presenting their journals to potential readers in a personal, direct way.

### Direct subsidy and accountability

Funders interested in establishing overall indicators of success for journals should take into account not only material factors, but also the intellectual nature of the journal and its potential readership.

In his concluding remarks, Ralf Dahrendorf warned against the danger of nostalgia for the role journals played in the old closed societies and stressed their continued importance as places for initiating debate. He also stressed that the contributions from speakers in the West made clear that the so-called "free market" was not nearly as market-like as it appeared, in view of the many forms of both direct and indirect subsidy which existed to support quality publishing. There would continue to be a place and a need for various forms of subsidy for journals.

# WORKSHOP FOR LITERARY TRANSLATORS, JUNE 1994

A workshop for literary translators was held on 11–12 June 1994, at the Oud-Poelgeest Estate in Oestgeest, the Netherlands.

## AIMS

The main aim of the workshop was to examine the position of the literary translator in various European countries, with a special emphasis on the "smaller" countries.

## ORGANISATION

The workshop was organised by the Stichting Nederlands Fonds Voor Midden- en Oosteuropese Boekprojekten (the Dutch Fund for Central and East European Book Projects), on the basis of a programme initially devised by CEEPP, and funded by the Prins Bernhard Fonds.

## STRUCTURE

The workshop took as its premise the importance of translators in disseminating and interpreting the literature and scholarship of different nations, and focused especially on their role in bridging the cultural gaps created by the post-war division of Europe. Its purpose was to discuss the professional problems faced by translators in both Western and Central and Eastern Europe, and to explore ways of overcoming them. Participants included translators from fifteen European countries, and representatives from the Dutch Ministry of Culture, the Dutch Fund, and the Obor Foundation (USA).

The problems discussed fell into the following broad categories:

(1) the practical difficulties experienced by translators in carrying out their work: e.g. in gaining access to information on new publications, or making arrangements to visit the country of their "target" language;
(2) the difficulty of persuading publishers to undertake the cost of translations, where the work in question is likely to have a small readership, and the consequent need for grants or subsidies;
(3) the absence or decline of university teaching, and hence of trained specialists, in the languages of the smaller European nations, and the greater difficulty therefore of presenting their literary or scholarly works elsewhere;
(4) the low status accorded translators in many countries, with poor financial rewards, and little or no social security or legal protection, so that many specialists are deterred from entering the profession.

In the course of the two-day workshop a number of suggestions were made for alleviating these problems, and these were incorporated in the following formal conclusions and recommendations.

## CONCLUSIONS AND RECOMMENDATIONS

Bearing in mind the twin goals of seeking greater mutual understanding among European cultures, and maintaining and promoting linguistic and cultural pluralism in Europe, this conference recognises:

(1) the importance and professional status of literary and scholarly translators, who play a key role in presenting and interpreting diverse cultures to one another;

and calls for:

(2) active attention to and support, on an institutional, national and European level, for the education of translators, and the mainte-

nance in universities of teaching in the languages and literatures of the smaller European nations;

(3) greater attention, on the part of funding bodies concerned with European culture, to the practical needs of translators, especially as regards travel, research facilities and access to information on publications; and for the inclusion of all the Central and East European countries in EU and other programmes designed to assist in this field;

(4) recognition of the continued need for grants and subsidies in the publication of literary and scholarly translations, especially in the Central and East European countries;

(5) protection of the professional rights and social welfare of translators, through greater access to information, the formation of professional associations, the promotion of relevant legislation and of respect for that legislation.

As immediate practical goals, this conference urges the relevant bodies:

(1) to establish a network of individual translators and representatives of translators' associations from both Western and Central/Eastern Europe, for the purpose of sharing information, and facilitating travel arrangements for translators seeking to visit the country of their specialisation;

(2) to investigate the possibility of establishing a number of stipends for translators seeking to make such visits, especially between the countries of Western and Central and Eastern Europe, and among the countries in the latter region;

(3) to explore ways of improving translators' access to information on publications, for example by creating, or researching existing bibliographies and databases of reference works and other sources of information.

(4) to develop a programme of grants to publishers of translations in Central and Eastern Europe, following the models of the Oxford CEEPP and Soros Foundations, this programme to include discretionary grants to meet the professional needs of translators;

(5) similarly, to develop a programme of grants to Western publishers and translators of literary and scholarly texts from Central and East European languages.

## TRANSLATION FELLOWSHIPS AT THE INSTITUTE FOR HUMAN SCIENCES (VIENNA), 1987–95

**1987/1988**

Pawel Hertz (Poland)
Jacob Burckhardt: *Die Zeit Konstantin des Großen*
Warsaw, PIW, 1992

**1988**

Jacek Baluch (Poland)
Jan Patocka: *Who are the Czechs?* and *Selected Writings*
Bratislava, Kalligram, 1995

**1988/1989**

Susanna Roth and Peter Sacher (Switzerland and Germany)
Ladislav Klima: *Postmortalien*
Berlin, Sirene, 1993

**1989**

Zoran Djindjic (Yugoslavia)
Edmund Husserl: *Die Krise der europäischen Wissenschaften und transzendentale Phänomenologie*
Belgrade, Decje Novine, 1991
Gabor Berenyi (Hungary)
Edmund Husserl: *Die Krise der europäischen Wissenschaften und transzendentale Phänomenologie*
Budapest, Atlantisz, 1995

**1989/1990**

Susanna Roth (Switzerland)
Jakub Deml: *Totentanz*
Richard Weiner: *Geschichten*
Leipzig, Reclam (in Kopfbahnhof, Almanach 5, and in Weiner "Der gleichgültige Zuschauer"), 1992
Jindrich Chalupecky: *Jakub Deml: Eine biographische Studie*

**1990**

Stanislaw Burakowski (Poland)
Georg Simmel: *Auswahl von Essays*
Andrzej Borowski (Poland)
E.R. Curtius: *Europäische Literatur und lateinisches Mittelalter*

**1991**

Jiri Pachar (Czech Republic)
Ludwig Wittgenstein: *Philosophical Investigations*
Prague, Filosoficky ustav AV CR, 1993
Dorota Lachowska (Poland)
Edmund Burke: *Reflections on the Revolution in France*

**1992**

Ryszard Nycz (Poland)
M.H. Abrams: *The Mirror and the Lamp, Romantic Theory and the Critical Tradition*
Warsaw, Instytut Badan Literackich PAN
Imre Kertesz (Hungary)
Ludwig Wittgenstein: *Vermischte Bemerkungen*
Excerpts printed in *Orpheus* (1992/III/1) and *2000* (June 1992)
Budapest, Atlantisz, 1995
Miroslav Petricek (Czech Republic)
G.W.F. Hegel: *Wissenschaftliche Logik*
Jacques Derrida: *Selected Texts*
Bratislava, Archa, 1993

**1993**

Jerzy Jarzebski (Poland)
Michel Foucault: *Les mots et les choses*, 1995
Gyorgy Petri (Hungary)
Karl Popper: *Logik der Forschung*
Budapest, Europa-Verlag, 1996
Irina Kjuldjieva-Fayon (Bulgaria)
J.L. Talmon: *Political Messianism*
Sofia, Center for the Study of Democracy, 1995
Malgorzata Lukasiewicz (Poland)

Friedrich Nietzsche: *Unzeitgemäße Betrachtungen*
Vorabdruck ausgewählter Kapital, Teksty, 1994
Krakow, Znak, or Poznan, Verlag A5, 1995
Otto Vochoc (Czech Republic)
Sigmund Freud: *Traumdeutung*
Prague, Hynek, 1995
Jiri Stromsik (Czech Republic)
Elias Canetti: *Masse und Macht*
Prague, Andrej Müller – Arcadia, 1994

**1994**
Eva Galandova (Slovakia)
Istvan Bibo: *A kelet-europai kisallamok nyomorusaga – Die Misere der osteuropäischen Kleinstaaten*
Bratislava, Stimul (Comenius University)
Jan Garewicz (Poland)
Martin Buber: *Gog und Magog*
Torun, Comer, 1995
Marta Herucova (Slovakia)
Erwin Panofsky: *Tomb Sculpture*
Bratislava, JM Press, 1995
Maria Kajtar (Hungary)
Golo Mann: *Deutsche Geschichte des 19. und 20. Jahrhunderts*
Budapest, Balassi, 1995
Hans-Henning Paetzke (Germany)
Eva Forgacs: *Bauhaus, A demokracia anatomiaja (Geschichte des Bauhauses)*
Frankfurt, Neue Kritik, 1995
Pravda Spassova (Bulgaria)
Leszek Kolakowski: *Main Currents of Marxism*
Sofia, Izbor
Arunas Sverdiolas (Lithuania)
Hans-Georg Gadamer: *Kleine Schriften. Eine Auswahl*
Vilnius, Baltos Lankos

**1995**

Silvelia Ruxandra Demetrescu (Romania)

Alois Riegl: Selected texts from *Historische Grammatik der Bildenden Künste; Stilfragen; Spätromische Kunstindustrie; Die Entsehung der Barockkunst in Rom*

Bucharest, Meridiane

Zdenka Kalnicka (Slovakia)

Paul Ricoeur: *Interpretation Theory: Discourse and the Surplus of Meaning*

Umberto Eco: *Interpretation and Overinterpretation*

Bratislava, Archa

Robert Kiss Szeman (Hungary)

Jan Patocka: Selected Texts

Bratislava, Archa

Stefan Nemeth (Slovakia)

Jan Patocka: Selected Texts

Bratislava, Kalligram

Andrzej Przylebski (Poland)

Georg Simmel: *Philosophie des Geldes*

Poznan, Rebis

Kornel Steiger (Hungary)

G.S. Kirk/J.E. Raven/M. Schofield: *The Presocratic Philosophers*

Budapest, Atlantisz

Igor Zabel (Slovakia)

Michael Baxandall: *Painting & Experience in Fifteenth Century Italy: A Primer in the Social History of Pictorial Style*

Ljubljana, SKUC

# *Publishing in the Visegrad countries in 1994: A report with suggestions for Western help*

RICHARD DAVY

## INTRODUCTION

> "Books are Europe's oldest common cultural asset; translations are the key to Europe's cultures. Private in origin but public in effect, geared to the market but produced with an idealism which often runs counter to market forces: down to the present day, books are the most resilient and at the same time the most sensitive product of European culture.
>
> "They need support throughout Europe. What is required is not interference in the running of the book business along private enterprise lines but assistance wherever books make a contribution of their own to a common Europe."[1]

As communism was collapsing, someone drew a balloon on a portrait of Karl Marx that made him appear to be saying: "Sorry, folks, it was just an idea." Whether ideas drive history or are merely harnessed by politicians the harm they can do needs no further demonstration. Europe has brewed up some of the worst as well as the best ideas in human history, and intellectuals have too often contributed to the continent's appalling history of wars and mad ideologies. In some areas they are still at it, concocting false versions of history to justify aggression or confusing the preservation of old cultures with ethnic nationalism.[2]

That is the first of four good reasons why we should help publishers in Central Europe. Good ideas will not always drive out bad, but they have a better chance competing in a "common market of the mind". A healthy book trade that reconnects the severed intellectual life of Europe should foster free trade in ideas and thereby contribute to the avoidance of war.

A second reason for helping is that the educational systems of today produce the elites of tomorrow. To invest in their enlightenment, professional skills and Western contacts by broadening their range of reading matter is also to increase the chances of peace and prosperity. At the moment the schools and universities of the area are badly underfunded and still struggling with the legacy of ideological control. Outside help for books and journals will help them catch up more quickly with Western Europe and assist rising generations to develop those skills in selecting, comparing and evaluating that were discouraged under socialism.

A third reason for helping is to buy goodwill among the intelligentsia of the new democracies. People remember those who have helped them through difficult times. Western policies towards Central and Eastern Europe since the fall of communism have been worse than disappointing. Historians will not be kind to the confusion with which Western governments responded to this extraordinary moment in European history: their shallow thinking, their self-interested promotion of national interests, their generous funding of consultants of mixed ability in glossy hotels, their slowness in opening the doors of the European Community or even defining conditions for entering, and their shameful cowardice in the face of protectionist pressures.

Although these failures are being gradually remedied, the disappointment remains deep and lasting. Some of it is the result of exaggerated expectations but much of it is justified. All the more important, therefore, in partly redeeming this sorry record, have been the efforts of non-governmental bodies and private foundations together with some Western publishers. They have provided limited but invaluable help for cultures struggling to survive the withdrawal of subsidies, the impoverishment of the intelligentsia and the inroads of commercialism. Patchy, quirky and doubtless misdirected though some of this help has been, it has nurtured small areas of intellectual activity that have fertilised others and helped to create networks of like-minded people whose contacts will help knit together the severed continent. In the process, some small pockets of gratitude have been created.

There is also a fourth reason for helping, less easy to justify or define. Central Europe is not a culturally retarded area begging for enlightenment from its more advanced neighbours. Such attitudes rightly provoke charges of intellectual colonialism and condescension. The nations of the area have their own rich cultures that have been warped and battered but also enriched by the experiences they have been through. They have a deficit to make up in publishing because of the political controls under which they have lived, but they have something to teach Western Europe about the human condition, human rights, the abuse of power and the history of the continent. Their experiences and the lessons they have learned are part of Europe's history and will gradually be shared, providing a mirror in which the West will encounter new images of itself. Helping cultural trade in both directions should, therefore, enrich the intellectual life of the entire continent.

Meanwhile, the transition is not yet over. Communism did not destroy culture. It tried to buy and control it with lavish subsidies. The effect was to corrupt, distort and suppress creative work but also to stimulate it. Large numbers of people were able to write books, plays and essays, make films, act and play music. Books of a limited range were cheap, plentiful, and widely read. So much creative activity could not be entirely contained within official limits. It spilled over into forbidden areas and fertilised the ground from which opposition sprang. In the 1970s and 1980s it helped to provoke the emergence of strong counter-cultures with their own illegal publishing industries, secret seminars, Poland's "Flying University" and networks of international contacts. All of these did much to preserve civil societies and create centres of moral authority that challenged the regimes and stepped in when they crumbled. By simultaneously fostering culture and repressing it the regimes prepared the way for their own destruction.

When freedom came it released a huge wave of publishing, mostly of home-grown and foreign writings that had been banned by the communist authorities – works by opposition writers, biographies and memoirs of democratic politicians, books on prisons and interrogations, and Western literature on totalitarianism, such as George Orwell and Karl Popper, that had been available only in samizdat. Close behind came another and larger wave from the West – romantic fiction, crime, horror, science fiction, pornography, coffee table picture books, coloured encyclopedias, works on feminism, do-it-yourself and above all business studies, the new bibles promising salvation through riches.

Intellectuals soon faced a double shock. Many of those who had been in opposition briefly tasted political power, only to be elbowed aside by professionals, often from the very apparatus that had oppressed them. Then they found their incomes, their status and their influence dwindling. The free market for which many of them had yearned began to cut away the subsidies and easy wages on which they had lived. Few had expected market forces to affect their privileges so directly because culture had for so long enjoyed special status. "The idea that writers and sculptors would be liable to the same tax as joiners or car mechanics seemed outrageous."[3] Dismay afflicted both the old guard who hoped to cling to some of their benefits and opposition figures who believed they should come into their subsidised inheritance. Culture seemed almost more threatened by market forces than it had been by political control.

The intelligentsia – not just intellectuals but broad swathes of the educated classes – had long seen themselves as the heart and soul of Central Europe, battered and corrupted by politics, decimated by purges and emigrations but still the custodians of national identities, the repositories of moral values, the primary source of ideas and setters of national agendas. Feared and wooed by the regimes, they conducted the political debates for which there were no democratic institutions. Now they found themselves again on the defensive, not only their incomes shrinking but their influence sliced away by consumerism, democratic politics, international competition and the huge proliferation of new books.

Although their buying power will increase again as money comes into the educational system, where many of them work, they will probably never recover the social status and influence they once had because of the lasting changes that are taking place in society and income distribution. Their reading has begun to diverge from that of the general public, and an element of social cohesion has also been lost because there are so many books on the market that people are no longer drawn together by reading the same books. This deeply affects the book trade. "Reading is not a measure of social prestige any more; it has become a private matter of an individual," writes Janusz Ankudowicz of the Polish National Library,[4] lamenting that the elites have lost their power to guide taste.

Some fear that this will kill off the dedicated publishers of quality books. They are almost certainly wrong, but it is true that the transition to market conditions has been especially difficult for the book trade because social and economic changes have come together, impoverishing the buyers, on whom serious publishers depend, at the same time as raising the costs of production to near world levels. The huge, lumbering state publishers, accustomed to turning out long runs of officially approved books regardless of demand, and mostly enjoying monopolies in their allocated sectors, have had to slim down, diversify and respond to the market or go bankrupt. Opposition publishers who had worked illegally from flats and basements have had to learn to organise, pay taxes (sometimes) and operate openly in the marketplace without the guaranteed readership of the samizdat circuit. Foreign competition has been a new challenge for both types of publisher, and foreign investment both a help and a threat.

State distribution networks have mostly collapsed and many bookshops have gone out of business. Others are reluctant to sell anything that is not snapped up within a couple of weeks. Postal services are too expensive and inefficient to make mail order an attractive alternative. Libraries and educational institutions have found themselves without the money to buy new books, maintain subscriptions to foreign journals or introduce modern technology. Even basic information on the book trade is lacking. In some countries it is still very difficult for anyone, including booksellers, to find out what books are available.

Then there is the complex problem of new legislation on rights. Under the old system rights belonged to authors, who were paid by wordage and print runs rather than by sales. Publishers were granted only limited rights to publish in the original language and their contracts were limited by print run and short time periods, without any provision to generate further earnings from the sale of additional rights, such as translation rights. It has taken time to understand that publishers, who are now taking risks in market conditions and facing international competition, need better protection and more rights. That battle is still being fought. Much new legislation in the region does not permit full assignment of copyright to a publishing house, which reduces the publisher's incentive to exploit a publication fully.

Adjustment has been made even more difficult in most countries by confusion over the proper role of government. Fearing commercialisation as much as government control, publishers have often been unsure what they wanted. Should books and journals receive subsidies and tax breaks or be treated as just another industry? If subsidies, how are these to be allocated in ways that do not disguise new forms of political control? The writers and intellectuals who entered government in the first wave of free elections found their personal feelings for books in conflict with the new ideology of the free market. There have been strenuous battles, as in Western countries, over whether Value Added Tax should be levied on books. Paradoxically, the return of post-communist parties to government in three of the Visegrad countries has brought a somewhat more sympathetic attitude to book subsidies, although perhaps with a hidden agenda of trying to reassert a measure of control, or at least achieve partisanship in the allocation of subsidies.

Some publishers made a lot of money in the first wave of freedom, either by putting previously forbidden work quickly on the market or – with more lasting results – by riding the wave of imported popular literature. But many serious publishers failed, and nearly all are still struggling. Those who survive do so by a variety of tactics. Some seek out Western best-sellers to support the rest of their lists. Some learn how to restructure. Some dedicate themselves to the new skills of applying for subsidies from governments and foreign foundations.

Yet fears for the indigenous book trade can be as exaggerated as predictions of the death of culture. Even a fully Westernised model does not destroy small publishers or quality books. For every conglomerate takeover in the West, another small publisher pops into the market. In Britain, 80,000 titles were published in 1993, 10 per cent more than in the previous year. True, Western economies are much richer. Yet publishing in most countries attracts dedicated people, professional and semi-amateur, who are willing to bring out serious books at a loss, even if it makes no sense to their accountants. That has always been one of the strengths and peculiarities of publishing. There is no reason why it should not also be true in the states of Central Europe, provided they enjoy reasonable economic growth.

The following sections look at each country in turn before reaching some general conclusions.

## POLAND

"I spend all my time applying for funds, not dealing with books," says Jerzy Illg wearily. He is Editor-in-Chief of Znak Books in Krakow, a publishing house with a proud history of representing the independent Catholic intelligentsia. Znak puts out a monthly and a weekly paper as well as books. Under communism it was frequently harassed by the authorities. Now it fights the different pressures of commercialism and competition.

Although Znak represents only one of several elements in the Polish intelligentsia, it exemplifies the plight of small, serious publishers struggling to maintain not only their production but their role in society. Its print runs are dropping, and it has resorted to putting out a series of paperbacks under a different imprint so as not to compromise its image. It cannot make a profit on runs of less than 4,000, and that is a lot by today's standards. Between a third and half of its titles receive some kind of subsidy from the Ministry of Culture, the French or German governments, the Robert Bosch Foundation, and others. But profits are still elusive.

Znak also suffers from the gap that has opened up between

secularism and conservative Catholicism. Space for the type of independent liberal Catholicism represented by Znak is shrinking, along with the incomes of its regular readers. The circulation of its weekly paper, *Tygodnik Powszechny*, has dropped from 100,000 in 1989 to below 30,000, although it may now be stabilising or even rising slightly.

The pressures on serious publishers are the result of social as well as economic change, and probably reflect a major break with history. Poland has a long tradition of defending its language and culture under partition and foreign occupation. A National Education Commission was created in 1773 to replace Catholic schools with a state system. Towards the end of the nineteenth century a movement of young people arose to defend Polish language and culture, sending teachers like missionaries around the land. As Norman Davies writes in *God's Playground*, "the typical Polish 'patriot' of the turn of the century was not the revolutionary with a revolver in his pocket but the young lady of good family with a textbook under her shawl."[5]

These idealists were largely successful in neutralising both German and Russian influences by building a huge informal educational system with secret libraries, clandestine classes and the famous Flying University, later emulated by the opposition under communism. Under Nazism, too, when the intelligentsia was systematically decimated, Poles sprang to the defence of their culture by setting up secret presses and university courses.

Now members of the intelligentsia are asking whether Polish culture can resist the depredations and degradations of commercialism as successfully as it did the efforts of the foreign occupiers. Talking to Polish publishers, one gets the impression that the Harlequin series of cheap romances (Mills and Boon in Britain) has taken the place of the Russians, the Germans and the communists in Polish demonology. Where all three failed to destroy Polish culture, Harlequin is apparently succeeding.

But the question should surely be put differently. Under foreign occupation, Poland was fighting to preserve its existence as a nation. Now its existence is no longer threatened. Its borders are accepted and its people are among the most ethnically homogeneous in Europe.

Instead, Poland is facing much the same exposure to international commerce and global communications as other modern states, all of which are having to re-define the nature of sovereignty and cultural identity. The changing face of publishing is only one aspect of this new reality. It certainly contains threats but not, in the old sense, to the nation itself.

All the same, it is not easy for Poles conscious of their heritage to come to terms with the falling demand for serious books. Most painful of all is the declining interest in history, which enjoyed huge political significance for two centuries. This has caught former underground publishers by surprise and left many of the literary fruits of the new freedoms rotting in warehouses. If there was one branch of writing that used to seem the lifeblood of Poles it was history.

The cultural effects of changed reading habits have been noted by Halina Lambert. In the past, she writes, everyone read the same novels and could discuss them together. "Nowadays there are so many titles that it is not possible to read everything good on offer. A well-read person was, until recently, held in high esteem socially. But not any more. Now, when everybody reads at random, there is no opportunity to make references to books in conversations, and there is no longer any common ground for discussion." She was pleading for famous literary figures to restore this common ground by endorsing selected books or series.[6]

## Transition

Yet in many ways, the publishing scene is more dynamic and hopeful in Poland than in the rest of the Visegrad area. Poles have long been avid readers. They bought 300,000 copies of Umberto Eco's *The Name of the Rose*, 30,000 of *Pendulum* and more than 200,000 copies of Joyce's *Ulysses*. Queues of ordinary people jostled to enter the Warsaw Book Fair in the spring of 1994. If they were not all looking for Polish history they were certainly interested in much more than romantic fiction. The huge variety of books now on offer has spread interest more widely, and polls show that the percentage of people who do not read at all has diminished, reflecting an increase in occasional readers. At present, readers in this category tell researchers they cannot remember titles but "it had something to do with love". Harlequin again. But once they acquire the reading habit their interests may broaden. Indeed, some hopeful observers believe the tide of rubbish is already beginning to ebb, giving way to interest in popular science, self-help and foreign language instruction.

Polish publishing is helped by the size of the country. With a population of more than 38 million, plus Polish-speakers in Lithuania, the potential market for Polish language books is more than three times that for books in Hungarian, for instance, so print runs can be much longer.

Poland also gains from having been the most liberal of the Visegrad Four after 1956, with a much wider range of books available. Even former opposition figures such as Andrzej Rosner, now head of the Books Department of the Ministry of Culture, admits that the communist regime deserves credit for providing mass editions of relatively cheap books, excellent children's books, about 9,000 regular libraries and more than 29,500 library centres.

Moreover, after 1977 the regime found it lacked the nerve to suppress entirely a burgeoning underground press which produced thousands of titles a year for several million readers.[7] Culturally and intellectually, state control ended long before the end of communism. Several of today's publishers acquired their skills, enthusiasm and entrepreneurial spirit in that environment.

Nevertheless, the end of communism faced them with severe challenges as well as opportunities. State subsidies shrank along with political restrictions. The unwieldy printing presses of the large state firms produced poor quality books inefficiently, especially on short runs. In 1990 book prices increased by 1,000 per cent, in 1991 by 400 per cent, in 1992 by 120 per cent, yet they still remained several times lower than in the West.[8] A small private publisher needed to sell about 4,500 copies to break even, a large state publisher about 10,000.

Competition became stiffer with the legalisation of underground publishers and the proliferation of new publishers. In 1994 there were about 3,000 publishers registered, but not all were operational. Many published maybe two or three titles a year, leaving about 150 serious publishers, of which only 40–60 now have a significant place in the market. Life for all of them became more difficult as prices rose, the market shrank and the intelligentsia became impoverished. Books that would have sold 50,000 copies a few years before were starting to find only 5,000 buyers if they were lucky, or 2–3,000 if they were about politics.

At the same time there was a flood of popular books from abroad which earned huge fortunes for some publishers. Harlequin editions often sell 200,000 copies, and there has been a boom in all kinds of publications for women. With additional competition from video recorders and satellite television, both of which enjoy more owners per capita in Poland than in the rest of the area, quality publishers started to feel seriously threatened.

Their troubles were aggravated by chaotic distribution which meant that they could not even reach all their potential customers. Distribution broke down completely in 1990. The state-owned distributor, Skladnica Ksiegarska, went bankrupt in 1992, leaving millions of books unsold, including many classics. After 1989 several thousand private distributors sprang up,[9] but only 100 of any significance remain, and none has been able to cover the whole country. Dom Ksiazki, for instance, was a large state distributor with some 200 shops. Now still state-owned but expecting to be privatised, it has about 70 shops in and around Warsaw.

Most of the bookshops in the provinces went bankrupt and those that survived turned mainly to cheap romances, leaving quality literature to be sold in about 250 bookshops in the largest towns. Since about a third of the reading public lives outside cities, there is a substantial market lying beyond the reach of the present distribution system. Mail order is regarded as no solution because postage can exceed the price of the book. It is cheaper to send books from London than within Poland.

Public libraries also deteriorated sharply. There are about 9,300 public libraries and 30,000 school libraries. Only the National Library and 49 district libraries are financed by the Ministry of Culture and Fine Arts. The rest come under local governments, which are very short of funds. A few years ago the state stopped buying new books for libraries, leaving about 50 on survival money only. There are plans to put more money into libraries but the Ministry estimates that to buy new books for all libraries would cost more than $15 million a year. In 1992 foreign experts estimated that university and technical libraries needed $35 million for automation. The Mellon Foundation has meanwhile contributed funds for the automation of selected academic libraries.

## Information gap

The distribution system has been additionally weakened by lack of information. Andrzej Rosner estimated recently that only 10,500 titles out of a probable total of 20,000 a year were registered, so bookshops, libraries and publishers have not known what was available. Periodicals such as *Ex Libris* and *Notes Wydawniczy* contain partial information but often do not reach the provinces. The lack of information has been especially frustrating for eager young readers who see titles in the shops or read about them in journals but cannot get them from libraries.

The information gap should be closed fairly soon as the German Booksellers and Publishers Association has been providing computers and advice on setting up a register of books in print. At first only the 49 centrally administered libraries and at least one big bookshop in every main city will be on-line, but the system should spread, and will also be available in book form.

Pressure to register will be greatly increased because only books with an ISBN number will be spared VAT. Others could find themselves due for 22 per cent plus a substantial penalty. That threat, it is hoped, will diminish the number of cowboy publishers and bring about almost universal registration of books. There have already been long queues of publishers at the ISBN office hastening to register their books, but a full register was not in existence at the time of writing. Proposals have also been mooted for combined libraries and bookshops in vans that would travel to remoter areas, assisted by the government. Meanwhile, a new bill will require publishers to send 14 copies of each book to the 11 largest libraries.

Janusz Fogler, Vice-President of the Polish Chamber of Books and publisher of glossy and expensive art books, believes publishers should join up into five or six large groups to give them more power to face foreign competition. Otherwise, he says, Bertelsmann will take over. He complains particularly about late payments by distributors and shops. Going go court is useless because the shops go bankrupt before the money can be collected. What is needed, he argues, is about $20 million in capital to set up a private distributor. Inflation and devaluation make it very risky to take Western credits, so that it is sometimes cheaper to pay 60 per cent interest in Poland than 10 per cent in the West.

## Government policies

The government has not always been helpful. Heavy duties on imported paper and parts for printing machines made it cheaper for some commercial publishers to print abroad, at any rate until duty on paper was lifted in April 1993. Publishers pay 40 per cent income tax, plus a special tax on higher wages, which makes it uneconomical to dismiss workers and pay the remainder more. VAT on books was reduced to zero after a battle, but only until 31 December 1995, so efforts are continuing to make it permanent.

There is, however, money available for individual titles through the Cultural Foundation, an umbrella organisation formed by the Ministry of Culture, the Ministry of Finance, the Ministry of Education and the Committee of Scientific Research. The Cultural Foundation has had a troubled history and ceased operations for a time but it has now resumed under a new director. There is a long queue of applicants. In 1992 the equivalent of about $700,000 was spent on books and the same on about 50 cultural periodicals, national and regional, seven of which are fully financed, the rest partly. But Rosner estimates that five times that amount is needed.

Since the 1993 election the post-communist government has roughly doubled its budget for book subsidies through the Cultural Foundation, which now has about $2 million a year for books and other publications. It has supported about 70 cultural publications and 4–500 books. Grateful though publishers and authors are for the extra money, there is resentment that generous funding is also going to a new cultural weekly, *Wiadomosci Kulturalne*, which is seen largely as a home for the old guard. It is edited by Krzysztof Teodor Toeplitz, a former communist on *Polityka*, and funds are allocated directly by the Ministry because Rosner refused to provide them from his department's budget.

There is strong pressure among publishers to set up an independent Book Council but nothing has yet come of it. The envisaged council would consist of intellectuals and people with professional knowledge of the book market. It would disburse government funds and draw up a list of perhaps 2,000 books on which libraries could spend their money. "Otherwise," as one publisher observed, "if they are simply handed funds for book purchases, there is no knowing what they might spend it on. Harlequin, probably."

The government is starting new efforts this year to finance libraries. There was an idea of raising money by taxing certain types of popular book but the problems of distinguishing between "serious" and "popular" books were judged too complex. It was decided instead that the Ministry of Culture should tax all books and periodicals with print runs over 100,000, levying perhaps 0.5 per cent for a fund to allocate to libraries for book purchases.

## Stimulating demand

Publishers' interests are represented by the vigorous Polish Chamber of Books, founded in 1990, which sponsors the Warsaw Book Fair. Its President, Grzegorz Boguta, formerly a leading samizdat publisher who now runs PWN (see below), argues strongly for shifting subsidies from producers to consumers - that is, to libraries, scientific institutes and distribution networks. Subsidising the producer distorts the market, he says, because it enables publishers to produce books for which there is little demand. It also means that subsidised books can be sold cheaper than others, which makes booksellers less interested in them because margins are smaller.

One proposal under discussion is to allow institutions to buy at a discount, the difference being made up to the publisher and the bookseller after the book has been sold. This would rule out producing unwanted books for warehouses and eliminate unfair competition between subsidised and unsubsidised books because the buyer would be subsidised, not the book.

Even if this system were in place, and with, eventually, more money in the market, specialised books would still need help. For these, Boguta wants the Chamber of Books to become a clearing house for information on sources of funds. It would collect information and make it available in Polish to all publishers, who would be invited to seminars on how to apply. This would simplify life for publishers in search of support and increase transparency, reducing the jealousy that is sometimes caused by private arrangements between publishers and foundations.

## Rights

The Chamber is also pressing for improvement in the legal environment. The new law on copyright and neighbouring rights that came into force on 5 May, 1994, is regarded as providing too little protection for publishers.[10] It is likely to make Poland still ineligible to ratify the full Paris text of the Berne Convention and will not encourage publishers to invest in bringing authors on to the market. There are some welcome elements: protection has been extended to 50 years after the death of the author; penalties for piracy have been introduced with provisions for action under civil and criminal law; there is provision for the seizure of infringing copies and reprographic equipment; computer programs and audiovisual works are now protected; and neighbouring rights are protected for the first time.

However, moral rights remain perpetual, with the implication that responsibility would be handled by the state in the absence of heirs of the authors. A levy has been introduced on reprographic equipment but with the proviso that all revenue from the reproduction of printed material should be paid to the author with no share to the publisher whose interests have also been infringed. It is unclear exactly how the levy system will be administered.

The new law also retains very liberal provisions for reproduction and quotation of copyright material without permission or payment. These provisions would be considered detrimental to the commercial interests of authors and publishers in the West.

A further disappointment is the introduction of a requirement that users of works in the public domain pay a royalty of 5–8 per cent of gross receipts into a Fund for the Promotion of Creativity, to be administered by the Ministry of Culture in consultation with creative unions. This levy will hit publishers who established themselves in the early 1990s on the basis of free access to public domain works.

There is also a provision for a contract between author and publisher to be retrospectively renegotiated if the profits of the publishers are considered disproportionate, but it is unclear who would assess this. An author may also cancel a contract "for reasons of his or her vital creative interests", which further undermines the security of publishers. The law remains very imprecise on matters such as the extent of rights that can be granted and the territory and duration of the licence. The result of all these problems is that publishers are still unable to commit themselves as fully to their books as they would wish.

## State publishers

Poland still has several large state publishers that struggle to survive in the new market. One such is Panstwowy Instytut Wydawniczy (PIW), which specialises in philosophy, history and belles lettres. It publishes about 100 titles a year, of which half are translated. Although state-owned, and with the huge advantage of receiving free accommodation, it must otherwise fend for itself and pay taxes. It receives no government help except title by title.

Alojzy Kolodziej, Editor-in-Chief, says the firm badly needs subsidies for books with small print runs. He wants to publish a collection of 70 titles on Polish literature. He has money for seven of these from the Cultural Foundation but each year he has to negotiate for more. There is no political interference except for books that are subsidised, which have to be approved by the Cultural Foundation. Help is limited to Polish books. For translations he turns to the Stefan Batory Foundation or foreign embassies, but 1994 has been especially difficult.

Like many Polish publishers, and others in Central Europe, he complains bitterly about the role of literary agents and sub-agents, mainly Gerd Plessl of Munich and Jovan Milenkovic of Belgrade, who formerly worked together to build up a substantial business during the communist period. Foreign publishers, says Kolodziej, do not realise that these agents are no longer needed now that access to Poland is simple and money can be easily transferred. The agents take 9–10 per cent so they add to the cost of rights. For history books PIW is making direct contact with OUP and Longman but much fiction is still handled by agents. When Plessl's group split the complications became even greater, and some Polish publishers found themselves receiving two sets of bills.

There was a concerted effort at the Warsaw Book Fair to persuade foreign publishers to by-pass such agents, and Plessl himself seems resigned to losing business. Plans are now well advanced for the creation of two bodies, a rights centre at the Warsaw Book Fair in cooperation with the American Publishers Association and a standing copyright committee within the Polish Chamber of Books. However, Plessl and Milenkovic defend themselves by saying they provide a valuable service as intermediaries between two worlds that still do not understand each other. Large Western publishers, for instance, do not have the time to deal individually with thousands of tiny unknown Central European publishers, often operating from home and liable to go bankrupt at any moment.[11]

This is less of a problem for large educational publishers, such as Wydawnictwo Naukowo-Techniczne (WNT), which specialises in university and academic books, science and technology, monographs, and technical dictionaries. Although state-owned, and with no immediate prospect of being privatised, it operates in the market almost like a private company "except that we are honest about our taxes," says Aniela Topulos, General Manager. She confirms that there is a decline in academic publishing, and more competition, but "new publishers are not up to our quality and cannot have the same connections with universities. Many authors publish with us because of our reputation even if we pay less. We have professors advising us. New publishers try to cut corners."

WNT has expanded its range to include children's books and study aids. Some are successful, with large runs and good profit, but it tries to keep its old customers. In traditional areas of study such as science and engineering it can find Polish authors but about a quarter of its titles are translated, mostly on informatics. Within five years, says Topulos, echoing a frequent comment among publishers in Central Europe, the rising generation will have learnt English so there will be no need to translate so many books for universities.

Topulos is against subsidising consumers because she fears there would be too much bureaucracy involved. Subsidising the producer means estimating demand but an experienced publisher should have a good idea of the market, she claims. The Ministry of Education, of course, prefers subsidising publishers because it gives them more control.

"We have had no foreign help so far," says Topulos. "We applied to a German foundation but they could cover only the author's rights, and the rest of the cost of production was too high to bring a profit. We would welcome help because we sometimes want to publish books that are not supported by the Ministry of Education." There are some other sources in Poland, but not many. Each year there are books that WNT cannot publish because the Ministry's conditions are too narrow, and getting narrower all the time. This is because the Ministry of Education depends on the Finance Ministry, which insists on cuts.

WNT does not sell through normal bookshops but has its own specialised shops, some of which it supplies directly. It also tries to inform universities about its products, and sends free samples to teachers so they can recommend them to students. Even so, because of the poor flow of information on books in print, teachers have found themselves recommending books that are no longer available. The new book register should change that. Unfortunately, says Topulos, there is a grey market in photocopied books for students and so far the law has provided inadequate protection for publishers.

The market in schoolbooks is dominated by Wydawnictwa Szkolne i Pedagogiczne (WSIP), a large state-owned publisher whose employees resisted privatisation and have now won the support of the post-communist government. It publishes about 500–600 titles a year, buys rights for European and US textbooks and is moving into multi-media teaching aids. However, a few shadows are falling on its generally sunlit world. Its virtual monopoly is being challenged, and its largest wholesaler went bankrupt, owing it substantial sums.

## Non-state publishers

Among the largest private publishers is Boguta's PWN. Established 44 years ago to produce scientific books and students' textbooks, it was modernised after 1990 and then privatised in 1992 with the help of foreign capital. It brings out more than 400 titles a year and is developing extensive international contacts with American participation. It has bookshops in Warsaw, Wroclaw and Poznan, mainly for its own books, and also distributes to about 100 other bookshops that have contracts with it. About 10 per cent of its books rely on foreign help, while half make a profit without help.

Zofia Wiankowska-Ladyka, Editor-in-Chief of the Books Department, says the firm badly needs money for translations especially as there is a shortage of Polish authors in some fields that were suppressed or limited by the communists. For instance, Richard Pipes's *The Russian Revolution* has 700 pages and is very expensive. Pipes helped to get special concessions for the Polish rights and CEEPP supported the translation but the book will still lose money because it will sell less than the break-even figure of 10,000.

PWN has diversified into fiction and other areas but is not comfortable in the mass market and does not want to damage its image by publishing much outside its normal range of science, economics and history, primarily for universities. Its main problem is that universities are too poor to buy books. Better-funded higher education would be preferable to seeking help for individual titles, say the editors, but this will have to wait until the general economic situation improves.

Meanwhile, PWN spends a lot of time searching for funds. The Ministry of Education helps with academic text books, as does the Committee for Scientific Research. It has received grants from CEEPP, the Stefan Batory Foundation, the French embassy and other sources, but none from the US.

Struggling in the shadow of these large publishing houses are many smaller firms trying to carve out niches for themselves. One such is Wydawnictwo A5 of Poznan, a tiny non-profit-making publishing house run by Krystyna and Ryszard Krynicki. They bring out five or six titles a year, mainly poetry and essays that they feel are neglected by the large houses. Some of their authors are well known, such as Wislawa Szymborska, Stanislaw Baranczak and Adam Zagajewski; others are almost unknown, such as Wincenty Rozanski. Editions vary between 400 and 2,000 copies, although a new volume of Szymborska's poems ran to 13,000 and a new translation of Shakespeare's sonnets to 3,000.

Krystyna Krynicka says that their basic problem, as with all small publishers, is the lack of capital and the cost of credit. With inflation in 1994 at more than 32 per cent, interest can be ruinous. "Thus, when you start to publish a book you must have enough money available in advance to pay the author, plus typesetting, paper and printing. If the book sells well the money arrives in the course of nine months, by which time inflation has eaten up most of the profit."

Small editions are totally unremunerative and could not be published at all without subsidies, says Krynicka. "When we started work in 1991 we could break even at about 1,500 copies; now we cannot make a profit on 3,000 because the costs of printing and paper have risen so much. Paper was 70 cents a kilo in January 1994; today it is $1.5. As a result, we cannot afford a second edition of Shakespeare's sonnets, in spite of requests, since we would have to triple the price and that would be too much for the average purchaser." Printing abroad, as many large publishing houses do, is not an option for small editions.

Copyright fees are another problem. "Western publishers often ask outrageous fees even for a single poem and do not make allowances for Polish conditions. When a small poetry book costs $3 here it is a lot in proportion to an average monthly salary of $200, and most of our readers are members of the intelligentsia who earn less than that."

Taxes are also painful, particularly a tax on unsold stock, which drives publishers to destroy unsold books. In the quality market, where a book may sell slowly over several years, this is very damaging. Finally there is the familiar nightmare of distribution. "In the whole of Poland there is only one wholesale firm which specialises in our type of book," says Krynicka. "The larger wholesalers will not handle books that do not make quick profits." This problem is exacerbated by delays in creating a modern information system.

## Journals

Serious journals are struggling alongside books. *Res Publica Nowa*, formerly an underground periodical with a devoted following, now has to fight for readers in a crowded marketplace. It is, however, unique in being truly independent of political or religious bias. Marcin Krol, the editor, says he will give space to any opinions except those of radical nationalism or old-style socialism. He wants to maintain a sense of intellectual continuity, and is against rubbishing everything about the past: "Many people and groups in our new society think that everything old should be chucked away, but decent thinking continued even in bad times, and its quality was sometimes better than now."

About half of each issue is devoted to a single theme such as political corruption or why a constitution is necessary. Krol has found, however, that readers now find politics boring and respond more eagerly to discussion of themes such as joy, melancholy and the significance of speed in modern life.

Circulation is healthy by Western standards but profits are a long way off. "We print 4,600 copies and sell around 3,300, including 900 by subscription. One of the mysteries of the distribution company is that it always sells about half what we supply. If we supply less it sells less. The surplus seems necessary so that we can be visible in kiosks. Unsold copies are used for promotion or sold cheap to students."

In spite of its relatively large circulation, *Res Publica Nowa* covers only 30 per cent of its costs, largely because it sells for the equivalent of about $1, a ridiculous price for a substantial monthly journal. But its readers, believes Krol, could not afford more. The Stefan Batory Foundation covers half its losses and will continue to do so through 1995. The rest is gathered from other sources including, until recently, CEEPP.

*Zeszyty Literackie*, another struggling journal of very high quality – perhaps the best of its type in Central Europe, according to experts – occupies a different niche. Edited by Barbara Torunczyk, it is a quarterly devoted to literature and the arts. It deliberately avoids direct discussion of politics, as it has done since it was started in Paris in 1983 by a remarkable group of intellectuals who happened to be there when martial law was imposed and saw the need for a publication to represent the new wave of emigrés. CEEPP supported it for much of its existence and both encouraged and helped fund its phased "return" to Poland after 1989. After moving back to Warsaw, its circulation fell slowly but may now have stabilised or even risen. The real costs of each issue are much higher than the price but it does not dare charge more because its main readers – students and teachers – are too poor. It receives some support from *Gazeta Wyborcza*, edited by Adam Michnik, which helps with production and publicity, but the relationship is felt as a potential threat to its independence. The Stefan Batory Foundation pays half the cost of library subscriptions, which is a big help.

The passing of CEEPP worries Torunczyk not only because she will miss the money: "CEEPP understood our problems; we need to maintain contacts abroad and read foreign journals if we are not to become isolated and provincial. These costs are beyond normal editorial and production costs."

## Conclusions

There is a fizz about Polish publishing that augurs well for the future. There is a plethora of ideas for improving the book trade, and plenty of people with the courage to promote them. Determination to get away from subsidising single titles is greater in Poland than in the other Visegrad countries. But changes are still raking the system, and the struggle is not easy for many serious publishers, large and small.

Ryszard Grabkowski, Executive Director of the Polish Chamber of Books, says that the situation is now far better than a few years ago. If foreign foundations stopped providing money, alternatives would be found, he claims. He feels that small publishers can be spoiled if they are helped too much. They must take risks or lose touch with demand. He is not happy about people in distant places deciding what books ought to be published in Poland. If there is foreign money available, he asserts, it should be spent not on supporting individual titles but on technical assistance, particularly for information and distribution systems.

Even the time for advice and seminars is past, he argues. Poland is now ready to be treated as a serious market. It particularly wants direct contact with American publishers, unhampered by agents and sub-agents. He claims that the new copyright law, despite its shortcomings, removes the last barrier to normal trade (others disagree), and that Poles have the entrepreneurial spirit to seize opportunities.

His attitude reflects the pride that contributes vigour to Polish publishing, but he glosses over some of the difficulties that hinder the production and distribution of serious books, particularly by small publishers. There is no doubt that a number of good books and journals would be lost if foreign assistance dried up before other types of support were in place.

## HUNGARY

A decade ago the Christmas tree in an educated Hungarian household was likely to be surrounded by books. Now, if there is money for anything, the gift-wrapped packages are more likely to contain Japanese gadgets. Books were plentiful and very cheap under communism. Controlled though they were by the inconstant whims of nervous politicians, they provided the intellectual stimulus and imaginative escape that the system discouraged in other departments of life. Hungary survived as a literate, even literary, nation, and intellectual life remained alive both inside and outside the permitted boundaries.

The end of communism came fairly smoothly after 20 years of economic reforms and expanding intellectual freedom. Yet the publishing trade was singularly unprepared. Life had been easy for those who did not press too hard against the limits of official tolerance. Publishers fulfilled their plans regardless of demand and were paid accordingly. Hugely overstaffed, they could allow one editor to be responsible for as little as one title a year, even though editing in the Western sense was minimal. Nor was there any need to learn Western skills in commissioning, marketing and negotiating with authors.

The creative intelligentsia led a sheltered if restricted life, wooed by the Kadar regime with privileges and a licence to criticise certain aspects of the regime. The bounds of toleration increased erratically as ideology died. By the late seventies the regime was concerned more with the sensitivities of the Kremlin than with the substance of debate in intellectual circles. Those who stepped out of line were dealt with fairly leniently; if sacked they would generally be found other means of making a living, albeit less comfortably. Academics who did not openly challenge the system were virtually guaranteed publication of their books, the quantity determined by their status in the hierarchy. Paid by the word, they could be luxuriantly prolix.

## Transition

Thus the freedom for which intellectuals had yearned brought shocks when it came. It had the paradoxical effect of jeopardising the supply of good books as well as ending a way of life. Subsidies dried up, production costs rose to near Western levels, yet prices had to remain in realistic relation to low incomes, even though some of them tripled. New private publishers proliferated to exploit the boom in previously forbidden work. Competition increased for the dwindling purchasing power of readers, driving some publishers into bankruptcy, some on a frantic search for domestic and foreign subsidies, and others on the trail of lucrative best-sellers. Small amateur publishers led a mayfly existence, appearing and disappearing almost by the day, often putting out no more than one or two titles a year, sometimes profitably, sometimes not.

As in Czechoslovakia and Poland, the first flood of new books was devoted to filling the black holes in the nation's history: the Stalinist period, the camps, the revolution of 1956 and relations with the Soviet Union. Once this demand had been satisfied, interest in history waned and readers turned to exploring the vast new array of popular fiction, romance and pornography that poured in from the West. They were somewhat less interested in the wave of Catholic and nationalist books encouraged by the conservative regime of Jozsef Antall. In the meantime the market became a jungle in which it was common to snatch authors, steal translations, ignore copyrights and plunder the assets of the former regime. Even armed force has been used in the book trade.

## Current problems

Considering these difficulties, Hungarian publishing has shown remarkable powers of survival. In 1993, 75 million books were printed, of which 85–90 per cent were supposedly sold (though this is questioned), and 7,500 new titles were published, according to government figures. There are now 1,300 publishing houses (some tiny), 800 printing houses and 70 distribution companies. The 1994 Budapest Book Fair attracted 80 Hungarian publishers and 2,000 trade visitors, including 500 from Western Europe.

Nevertheless, one finds few happy faces among publishers in Budapest. Most complain they cannot make a profit on runs of less than about 10,000, if then, because margins are too small to share with authors, printers and distributors. There is simply too little money in the economy. A new novel does well if it sells 2,000 copies at 500 forints, which is about half the cost price. Books on sociology or history sell for 800 forints, which is also less than half the production cost. The difference is made up from subsidies or commercial books if the publisher is skilful and lucky. Small publishers often manage better than large ones because they have lower overheads, but they can be guilty of shoddy editing and sharp practice.

The other principal lament concerns distribution. "We would be 50 per cent better off if we had a good distribution system," says Istvan Bart, President of the Publishers Association and Director of the Corvina publishing house, which specialises in illustrated books. The three big state distributors went bankrupt – some of them two or three times – after privatisation. There are now at least 40 small ones. Most of them are unreliable, and many are not real distributors but operators who collect a few books and drive them out to bookshops, often going bankrupt before they pay the publisher. Bart would like to set up a Chamber of Books with compulsory membership so as to strengthen the bargaining power of publishers, but other publishers and the government are horrified by the idea.

Many publishers look enviously at the Netherlands' Centraal Boekhuis, a modern distribution system set up by publishers and booksellers which handles some 36 million books a year. But the Hungarian Publishers' Association has no capital to set up such a system and, even if it had, the market might be insufficient to make the enterprise worthwhile. Moreover, Hungarian publishers would probably be unable to cooperate, as some of them ruefully admit.

Many bookshops have also closed, bringing down the total from 600 to below 300, of which only about 100 are serious establishments. Nobody knows the exact number. Half are still state-owned and waiting for privatisation, caught in a debate over whether they should be sold as chains or individually and to what type of owner. The new government is expected to be more pragmatic than the last.

Thus publishers spend too much of their time and manpower either distributing directly or working through firms that provide poor service and frequently go bankrupt with unpaid debts. Direct mail is sometimes used but is generally regarded as too expensive: a book costing 500 forints would cost 100 forints to post. The Bertelsmann Book Club distributes by post because it has the capital to create an efficient system and the marketing ability to charge realistic prices – sometimes higher than in the bookshops. Its marketing channels, including two shops in Budapest, will also open the way for other products, such as CDs and videos, which will spread the price of distribution.

Bertelsmann is resented because it creams off the best-sellers and potboilers with which Hungarian publishers would like to finance more serious books. But the manager of the Book Club, Dr Balazs Kratochwill, replies: "Publishers here are a bit lazy. There's been no real marketing for 40 years. They're simply not used to it. Too often they bought rights then didn't really sell the books."[12]

## The intelligentsia

The crisis in Hungarian publishing is bound up with the changing role and shrinking incomes of the intelligentsia. For much of the country's history, amid the shifting frontiers of Central Europe, language was the only definition of nationhood, so intellectuals were the custodians of the national identity, and their debates a substitute for democratic politics. The 1848 revolution started with the recital of poem on the steps of the National Museum. The revolution of 1956 grew in part from a literary movement. The end of communism was foreshadowed in intellectual circles long before it broke surface.

Today the talk continues but in a different context. Writers no longer need to write in code, and the closed coteries of cafés and discussion clubs have competition from open politics, where intellectuals must make real decisions. This does not mean that the intelligentsia have been depoliticised. "Populist" intellectuals were crucial in the formation of the Hungarian Democratic Forum, which led the coalition government after the election of 1990. "Urbanist" intellectuals, alarmed by the revival of nationalism, then rallied round the Alliance of Free Democrats.

Yet this continuing political engagement cannot disguise the fact that the intelligentsia are losing their position. They no longer set the nation's agenda and shape its values. The consumer society is creating new elites and defining status by money more than by politics or positions in the cultural hierarchy. The new rich have become the style setters and role models.

These changes affect the book market because the new rich are not great readers. The main customers for books – writers, teachers, students, bureaucrats – cannot afford to buy in the quantities they once did. A survey of the problem is being coordinated by the Institute of Sociology of the Hungarian Academy of Sciences, and the results are expected in 1995. "We know what is going on," says Laszlo Jakab Orsos, editor of *Nappali haz*, an intellectual review. "We reflect on it, we know that it is natural that we should not control society. We need to find our realistic place. We can penetrate society but cannot dictate any more. This affects the style of writers: you are not a leader any more, you are alone with your own troubled sensitivity."

## Struggling publishers

Among the more melancholy cases of troubled sensitivity is Gondolat, which used to be the major non-fiction house in Hungary, publishing 120 high-quality titles a year. Now, housed in the faded elegance of a crumbling palace, partly in the servants' quarters, it manages at best 30–40, mostly second or third editions, and is on the brink of collapse. It has dozens of books translated and ready for the printer but no funds. Some titles will therefore be snapped up by other publishers without payment when the publisher's rights expire after four years.

The biggest problem, says Miklos Hernadi, a senior editor, is finance. "There is a delay of 9–12 months before we get in our returns and every printer wants payments for production in advance or on publication. With inflation at around 25 per cent, that is a huge burden on any house." Gondolat has received no bank credits for the last three years, and could not afford them at 30–40 per cent interest, even though inflation brings this down to much less in real terms. These conditions produce too many "hit-and-run" houses with very small, often inexperienced staff, and a tendency to disregard royalties.

The editors at Gondolat realised some years ago that they must, as Hernadi puts it, "get off our cultural high horse and venture into low-brow publishing", but they found they lacked the experience to pick money-makers so they lost even more on these ventures. "None of our people were capable of reading these books and forming an opinion on them. We missed the train. We could not become a low-brow house."

So why not look more actively for foreign help? In the first place, says Hernadi, most foundations will help only private enterprise, and Gondolat is still state-owned. It would love to go private but cannot find a buyer and its staff are too poor to raise the money themselves. It does not own its building and has no assets except its unpublished manuscripts and the skills of its dwindling staff, recently diminished even more by the election of its director to parliament.

Secondly, much foreign help is targeted at translations and does not cover total costs. Moreover, books of the type for which Gondolat was renowned sell very slowly, and bookshops are reluctant to carry stock. After two weeks they get tired and return the books. Popular novels either sell in three days or not at all. The successful Hungarian publishers today have capital in the background from other business or foreign backers.

Should publishers form a cartel, as Istvan Bart recommends? The divisions in the publishing world are beyond repair, says Hernadi. You would always get some publishers trying to get better terms at the expense of others. Capitalism is still in its early, rough stage in Hungary, insufficiently regulated. The really tough publishers would never enter a cartel. They steal copyrights, manuscripts, books and authors. A few years ago there was an armed takeover of a store.

Legislation against late payments would be a big help, says Hernadi, who feels that the new coalition government is over-zealous in pursuit of the free market in order to impress the IMF. Culture cannot exists without state subsidies and some controls. "But my morality is someone else's censorship," he admits mournfully.

Somewhat more optimistic but also struggling is Europa, the largest literary publisher in Hungary, which was privatised about 18 months ago. Its list includes authors such as Günter Grass, Milan Kundera, Josef Skvorecky and Agatha Christie. It has also been able to add big money-makers such as Stephen King, Alexandra Ripley, E L Doctorow and Danielle Steel. Its employees bought it with an 8 per cent loan over eight years under a government programme. Its Director, Levente Osztovits, says not much has changed in the firm's way of life since privatisation except that it pays much more tax than ever before, plus social security at the same rate as for all industry. It has achieved some modernisation, including the recent introduction of bar coding.

Osztovits's main complaints are that prices are too low, except for luxury books, and that distribution is catastrophic. Libraries cannot afford to purchase, and customers often cannot find the books they want in shops. The firm has its own bookshop in Budapest but shops generally are expensive to run. Distribution is very time-consuming for a publishing house to do on its own.

Book-buying has declined largely because of the consumer society, says Osztovits. Two years ago Europa published 200 titles a year. In 1993 it was down to 127 and will put out about the same number in 1994. Most on its list are translations, half classical, half new. It does not depend heavily on foreign aid but if a book seems likely to attract a subsidy it applies. Even then it receives only part of the cost, maybe for translation or rights, and the amount is often insignificant. Generally it receives support for 8–10 titles a year. Without that support, the most important titles would suffer.

It lost two million forints on the first full Hungarian translation of de Tocqueville's *Democracy in America* although it received 800,000 forints from the USIA. After three years there are still 1,200 copies in the warehouse from a print run of 3,000, showing up the limited market for books of this type. One of the results of privatisation is that workers with a stake in the firm may grumble – as some did – that such a book is a waste of resources. It was possible only because of the dedication of editors to the image of the company. Since many of them are themselves poets and translators the policy survives, but competitors without this burden have an advantage.

The workers' complaints are, however, the result of outdated thinking. They should not be disappointed at selling 1,800 copies of de Tocqueville in a poor country of 10 million people. Per capita, this is probably much more than any Western market could absorb. The problem lies in the expectation – shared by bookshops and distributors – of selling all 3,000 at once. In modern conditions the need is for a system geared to slow but regular sales of important books. This requires more efficient storage and the ability to reprint easily and cheaply.

The acknowledged stars in the art of applying for subsidies are Tamas Miklos and Laszlo Kontler, founders of Atlantisz, a small publishing firm that also runs the Atlantisz Book Island in wonderfully central premises made available by the Eotvos Lorand University, where Miklos teaches. (Kontler teaches at the Central European University.) The Book Island is a combined showroom and bookshop, claimed as the first of its kind in East Central Europe, where customers can consult up-to-date catalogues, buy off the shelves or order any book in the field of social sciences.

As students in 1981, they started a journal called *Medvetanc* (Bear Dance), one of the lightly censored student journals of the time that enjoyed considerable freedom because the government had become too heavily indebted to the West to risk clamping down, particularly as the journal was quick to attract foreign attention. Sometimes individual issues were banned, such as a seminal collection of essays on reform in 1988, but the journal survived until 1989, when the editors closed it in the belief that it had fulfilled its function as a forum for free debate under communism.

Having accumulated experience and a circle of loyal readers and authors, Miklos and Kontler went into publishing. They founded Atlantisz in 1990, choosing the title to suggest a search for the lost continent of liberal intellectual Europe. Motivated by fears that the vacuum left by the collapse of the left would be filled by the nationalist right, they made it their mission to make available in Hungarian the classics of European liberal thought, in addition to some heavy German hermeneutics and existential philosophy. Since it was not possible to finance such books from the marketplace they created a foundation to raise money, receiving support from many sources, including the city councils of Budapest and Frankfurt.

In the first phase, Western governments, foundations and some Hungarian banks were eager to support them. Even Hungarian bureaucrats hurried to establish their cultural credentials. The mood has now changed, says Miklos, and funds are harder to come by. Atlantisz has 60 books ready for publication but no funds to print them. They include European and American classics and modern works. About 3 per cent of applications are successful. Nothing comes from the United States, and less now from Germany. The European Union suggests unsuitable titles, as do the Americans. CEEPP has been very helpful, and the Soros Foundation is extremely important because it has established a long-term commitment to Hungary.

Support for individual titles is not ideal, says Miklos. More useful is support for a series of books, such as modern classics, so that publishers can plan ahead. More money in the library system would also be an enormous help. For the present, direct support for publishers is the only feasible basis for help because it is transparent and builds up mutual trust. With any centralised or less intimate system money would go astray or be wasted by bureaucracies, he feels. The PHARE programme, for instance, is far too bureaucratic and works only through big institutions, which have their own bureaucracies that waste time and money. Foreign foundations need not necessarily spend scarce resources on local offices, says Miklos. What is vital is a long-term relationship of mutual trust and understanding such as existed with CEEPP.

The idea of subsidising the sale of books by paying the publisher a percentage for each book sold would certainly bring market pressures to bear, admits Miklos, but most publishers would regard it as too risky under present conditions.

He feels strongly that more should be done for Hungarian writers, or they will die out. They particularly need help in improving their chances on the international market. Most foreign help is for inward translation, which does not encourage interchange. For instance, Atlantisz is publishing a comparative analysis of the history and institutions of civil society, by Gabor Halmai, devoting special attention to how different countries limit freedom of opinion. Such a book deserves a wider readership, he feels, but needs outside funds for promotion.

The need to invest in the intellectual and spiritual future of the country has not diminished, says Miklos. The public could still turn hostile to the free market and democracy in the wrong intellectual environment. Already there are signs of an alliance between left and right against "Americanisation" and foreign capital. Nationalism is still a threat, and could become more dangerous if unemployment increases, particularly in the eastern part of Hungary, which is falling behind the western part.

## Success

As a contrast to struggling publishers dependent on aid it seemed worth looking at Kossuth Kiado. At the time of writing it was still owned by the Socialist Party but expecting to be privatised soon. In four years it has received nothing from foreign foundations. According to its President, Andras Sandor Kocsis, it receives neither capital nor subsidy from the party. In fact, he says, the party's main legacy was a stock of about 400 million forints' worth of unsaleable books about communism. Jealous competitors say Kossuth benefits greatly from its party connections, among other things by winning lucrative printing contracts. It has, however, made vigorous efforts to remain viable, cutting its annual production from more than 400 titles to 70–80 and its staff from some huge figure to 138 full-time employees, plus 80–90 part-time editors, translators and designers, and about 500 sales representatives. It also modernised its printing works by buying the presses of a bankrupt firm, so that it could take on contract work worth 50–60 million forints in 1994 as well as printing its own books. It maintains a retail network of 35 bookshops, nearly two-thirds of which are franchised family businesses, and is developing a computerised ordering system

It publishes mainly non fiction, philosophy, psychology, books for women and massive reference works, including the first Gypsy–Hungarian dictionary. It is giving serious attention to marketing CD-ROMs from Britain and America, distributing products from Time Warner, Bertelsmann and Quanta. Recently it signed a five-year agreement for exclusive rights to a Hungarian edition of a series for the National Geographic Society. Unlike many of its competitors it seems happy to draw on bank credits. Even if its party connections have been helpful, it appears to demonstrate that, with energy, capital and expertise, it is possible to succeed in some areas of serious publishing.

## Academic publishing

The travails of the academic sector are more specific and not susceptible to quick solutions. The more formal side is led by Akademiai Kiado, originally the publishing house of the Academy of Sciences and still the largest publisher of academic books and journals. About a third of its titles are requested by the Academy of Sciences, which makes up for its losses on these works at the end of each year. The rest of its titles are its own responsibility and include a wide range of academic works and reference books, particularly dictionaries. About a third of these are in foreign languages, mainly English, but it has had trouble finding partners to help with distribution. It does, however, cooperate with the Oxford University Press on English language teaching. It distributes partly through its own wholesale system, which requires personal connections and does not work well but is being computerised. Its editors complain that some foreign publishers, particularly Americans, show no interest in negotiating rights, and sometimes do not even answer letters, because royalties on Hungarian editions are too small.

Akademiai Kiado suffers from the malaise that afflicts the entire academic world. "Our strategy is survival," confesses Klara Takacsi-Nagy, Editorial Director. Scholars, students and libraries are all badly underfunded, and the educational budget is actually declining in real terms. According to a leading academic, "the Ministry of Finance is run by an accountant only interested in balancing the budget and satisfying the IMF." It is common knowledge that the Ministry of Culture and Education has little power.

A professor told me that all Hungary's academic libraries put together would not equal one at a second-ranking American university. Many buy only one example of a book and photocopy it without paying for rights. This is bad news for publishers and booksellers, but libraries are too poor to be worth suing, and in any case it is the only way they can supply their students and researchers. A new copyright law, still in preparation at the Ministry of Justice, would cut down photocopying, but if the libraries remain too poor to buy books it will merely make life still more difficult for students. The only satisfactory answer is to pump more money into the libraries and to work on schemes to increase purchasing power, such as student book vouchers.

This would also create more buyers for the work of struggling academic authors. At present, small allowances are available from universities, but this source is shrinking. There are also some funds available from the Academy of Sciences and various foundations. If an author can assemble this type of support he or she can then turn to a publishers such as Atlantisz or Akademia which may use their contacts to seek further grants from domestic or foreign foundations.

Money is not the only problem. There is a tradition of students working from set texts, verbal presentations and professors' notes. The idea that they should explore a wide variety of sources is still fairly alien. But change is delayed by the poverty of libraries, teachers and students. Teachers' notes, known as *scripta*, are often generated within universities, earning money for the authors and saving money for the students, but the system is unsatisfactory. Quality is variable, and each university tends to become an intellectual island, denied the traffic in material and the cross-fertilisation of ideas that should be a vital part of any country's educational system. This is particularly bad for research students, who need access to a wider choice of material.

Another result of underfunding is that teachers leave the profession, go abroad or seek attachments to other universities, since visitors are normally paid more than members of the staff. Recruitment of young university teachers is becoming a problem because of the low pay, although many find compensation in opportunities to spend time abroad.

At the level of secondary schools the supply of books is somewhat better, thanks partly to the energetic and imaginative work of the Ikon publishing house which turns out modern, well-produced texts, exam notes and European and Hungarian classics, incidentally also providing work for academics. Some of their books can also be used at undergraduate level.

Local authorities allow only 600 forints per child per year for books, although the list of required books costs several thousand. Families make up the rest, usually at great cost to themselves. Strangely, when some schools offered to buy the necessary books and lend them to pupils, parents resisted because it has been traditional to own books since the time when they were cheap and disposable.

Klara Takacsi-Nagy of Akademia is not keen on the principle of seeking outside support for individual titles. It is not always the right books that get help, she says. The best help for Akademia would be if libraries bought more books and more copies of each book, but this is unlikely in the near future. In the meantime Akademia is losing its monopoly as other large publishers reach out for the academic market and small publishers jostle to share the budget of the Academy of Sciences. Two have been founded by scientists who enjoy close personal connections with the Academy and are therefore well placed to get funds. The Central European University Press is also seen as competition for Akademia.

The second largest publisher in the academic sector is Szazadveg, directed with zeal and idealism by Janos Gyurgyak. He proclaims a policy of consolidating civil society and staying above the "mad clash between 'urbanism' and 'populism' - the confrontation that has traditionally split the Hungarian intelligentsia into two camps forever talking past one another." His original aim was to introduce West European political and cultural values into Hungary but his list has expanded to include wider areas of the social sciences, humanities, classical Hungarian works and world literature. He is now starting textbooks for universities in the social sciences, for which he is seeking financial support. He is also running a series of paperbacks of classical works, emulating Penguin.

Like Akademia, Szazadveg is in financial difficulties and was planning to cut its titles from 100 in 1994 to about half that in 1995. It was originally dependent mainly on the Soros Foundation but is trying to become self-financing and has set up a foundation of its own to seek donations. Gyurgyak lists his problems as high production costs, chaotic distribution, lack of information and falling demand for academic and semi-academic quality books. Some of his print runs for such works are high by European standards – up to 3,000 copies – but it is difficult to make a profit on less than 10,000.

Gyurgyak says he has almost stopped writing applications for individual titles because they were taking up about 90 per cent of his time while bringing only occasional successes. He received grants from CEEPP and then, after a talk with Timothy Garton Ash, realised that poorer countries to the East were now in much greater need.

He admits that funding the demand side would be better in theory, but under present circumstances, even if there were greater demand, publishers would be unable to meet it because they do not have ready cash for production and cannot afford to run up credit. The production cost of the paperback series is 500,000 forints, but a textbook can cost 5 million forints (though others dispute such a high figure), so publishers will still need subsidising for at least three years, and probably more, until the market begins to function. Rising generations are learning English fast, so the need to translate academic works will diminish, but at present there is still a huge need for Hungarian translations of scientific works, philosophy and sociology, which was badly neglected under communism.

## Information lag

A major problem for publishers and shops is the lack of reliable information on what books are available. In 1994 Szazadveg published a directory of books in print, but it will probably not repeat the experiment because the subsidy from the Ministry of Culture and Education is uncertain and in any case the experience has not been a happy one. Szazadveg believes the directory covered less than 70 per cent of books on the market because shops, publishers and distributors did not supply enough information. Unlike in Poland, there is no tax incentive to register books and many publishers do not bother. Gyurgyak also feels that the list should be published by someone other than a player in the market. He merely wanted to show that the job could be done by someone. On-line systems remain far off.

## Journals

Journals also have problems with distribution because few of them seem able to cooperate with each other or to link up with larger publishers to reduce overheads. *Nappali haz*, for instance, a quarterly arts review that sells around 2,000 copies, is not available in country areas except in two or three universities. Its editor dismisses postal subscriptions as unrealistic because the review's main readers are young intellectuals, students, teachers and artists who are thought unlikely to commit themselves to paying bills regularly. This may be too defeatist.

One of the best of the Budapest journals is *Budapesti Konyvszemle – BUKSZ*, also published in English as the *Budapest Review of Books*. A critical quarterly founded in 1989, it has a acquired a reputation for lively criticism. It prints 2,500–3,000 copies in Hungarian, covering the social sciences and humanities with book reviews and essays. Recent issues contained articles on ethnicity and nationalism, Hungarian history, Romanian anti-Semitism, Utopianism, anthropology and the European philosophical tradition. It, too, has distribution problems. It has tried to build up its own distribution network with other cultural journals but this has not been very efficient.

Feeling uncomfortably reliant on financial help from the Soros Foundation and CEEPP, it recently raised the price of its Hungarian edition to the equivalent of $1.20, with reductions for subscribers and students.

## Government policies

Government policies over the past few years have not been particularly helpful to the book trade. Publishers are granted no relief from corporation tax, and books have been charged 10 per cent VAT, rising to 12 per cent in 1995. There has been only slow progress towards providing an effective legal framework for the publishing trade and a law on non-profit institutions. Budgetary constraints are tighter under the present government. It inherited a large budget deficit from its predecessor, which was profligate in pumping money into foundations, publishing enterprises and individual pockets. The 1995 budget for book support is nominally the same as the previous year but, with inflation at 18.8 per cent in 1994, considerably lower in real terms.

Andras Torok, Deputy State Secretary at the Ministry of Culture, has compared publishers under communism to animals in a zoo, fed and fattened by their keepers.[13] When the system changed, the fences were taken down and the publishing world became a jungle in which wild animals struggled for life and killed each other. Government policy now, he says, should not be to feed some animals and put others on a diet but to provide fresh water so that all have an equal chance to survive. "Within 5–10 years we should move towards the concept of the safari park." There are only two immediate exceptions, he adds: the government should provide some support for "young animals" – that is, new publishers and writers – and should also save the jungle from dying out in certain regions, including Hungarian communities abroad.

An example of "fresh water" is the government's plan to buy a large bar code machine for the National Library and force publishers to use it. The government is also encouraging efforts to create a register of books in print on CD-ROM.

One of the most useful contributions that foreign foundations could make, he says, apart from continuing to support individual titles, would be to make available, through banks, low-interest loans to publishers, who cannot afford current rates of 30–35 per cent.

## Funding

The largest domestic source of funds for publishing is the Hungarian Book Foundation, an independent body established in 1992 under the auspices of the Ministry of Culture and Education. It gave out 100 million forints in 1994 and was hoping to spend 120 million in 1995. It is administered by a committee of 10 members delegated from various organisations and includes one member appointed by the Ministry who cannot be chairman. A publisher who puts in an application has to leave the room when his own application is discussed. After a somewhat troubled period, its new head is Istvan Lakatos, a poet.

Another source of help is the National Cultural Fund, of which Andras Torok is president. It has a book budget and supports Hungarian attendance at the Frankfurt Book Fair. Budapest publishers also receive help from the city government. There is a considerable amount of money in various Hungarian foundations of left and right, several funded from the pseudo-privatisation of the assets of the former Communist Party, much of which went into real estate and publishing. Some of these foundations support serious publications, partly to provide work for sympathetic journalists and more broadly to retain the sympathy and support of the intelligentsia.

The largest source of foreign money is the Soros Foundation, without which Hungary's intellectual life would be in a far worse state than it is. The Soros publishing programme was expecting to spend about 70 million forints in 1994 from a budget that has roughly kept pace with inflation over the years. The Central European University, with its own press, is a separate operation but coordinates with other Soros programmes.

Soros is also rare among foundations, apart from CEEPP, in promoting "East–East" cooperation, which is too often neglected. It has a periodicals programme that promotes meetings, study trips and the interchange of articles among journals in the former Soviet area. It also supports a monthly "Visegrad" section in four newspapers: *Gazeta Wyborcza, Narodna Obroda, Magyar Hirlap* and *Lidove noviny*. One of the few others in the field of "East–East" cooperation is the Institute for Human Sciences in Vienna, with its translation fellowships initiated as a joint venture with CEEPP and now co-funded by the European Cultural Foundation. Several of the translators on the Fellowship have been translating from one Central or East European language into another.

The French government is reasonably generous with subsidies for translating French works into Hungarian, normally leaving the choice of translator to the Hungarian publisher. The German government does the same through InterNationes and the Goethe Foundation, although projects can be cumbersome because they have to be negotiated through cooperative German publishers, who are not always easy to find.

The USIA provides money for translation from American into Hungarian but tends to push its own list of books, which is regarded as too limited and biased towards business studies. Akademia has not taken any of their political titles, saying they were of insufficiently high quality. The US government does not pay for rights because the money is not allowed to return to the US. The British government is widely criticised for providing no money for translating from English into local languages.

## Conclusions

With only a small language area to supply, Hungarian publishing can never be big business. Specialist books will always need support of some kind. Increasingly, certain university courses will come to be taught partly or mainly in English, as they are in the Netherlands and Scandinavia, because it will not be worth translating every required book into Hungarian. But demand for books and information of all sorts will be grow as new fields of study open up and students demand a wider range of reading matter.

At present, although the market is still chaotic and weak, a wide range of good books is available in Hungary, thanks to the dedication of publishers and their ability to generate support. But almost everyone agrees that putting forward single applications for single titles is inefficient, time-consuming, sometimes unjust and too insensitive to demand. Gradually, most of that system will have to be phased out.

One critical academic observer of the scene summed up his feelings as follows: "If the Ministry of Culture and other semi-public grant agencies would make library support dependent on opening modern students' libraries where most of the titles are available in several copies; if the students themselves were given an allowance to buy books for their exams; and if publishers could get advantageous loans for textbook publishing, then a workable system could be established. The problem is that for such complicated reforms it is hard to build a political constituency. All the actors on the scene – publishers, distributors, bookshops, libraries, students, teachers – are interested only in quick cash subsidies with no strings attached."

Until these attitudes and policies change, there is no alternative to continuing limited – preferably dwindling – support for individual titles. The educational system will remain underfunded for some time, and even when individual consumers have more money in their pockets they will not always spend it on serious books. For at least a few years, subsidies from outside sources will be necessary, and abrupt withdrawal would cause serious casualties.

Over the longer term the book trade will be best helped by better funding of libraries and the entire educational system, coupled with carefully targeted technical assistance for modernising libraries, distribution and information systems. On-line systems must await better telephone lines but in the meantime more effort could be devoted to showing publishers how they could gain from cooperative distribution and information systems. To be blunt, they need their heads knocking together.

World Bank funds are available in principle for an ambitious plan to produce a new generation of textbooks for all levels of education and to improve libraries by helping them with the purchase of new books and journals, automation, training schemes and the refurbishment of buildings. Very thorough studies have been made, funded through a Japanese technical assistance grant, but government changes and general disarray have so far held up agreement. (See concluding section.)

International Book Development, a London consultancy that has done studies for the World Bank and others, reckons that if total existing grants for books were transferred to students by means of credit or voucher schemes, a market equivalent to $7.5 million would be created immediately. If students added their own money demand could be worth more than $12 million, creating a reasonably attractive commercial market for publishers, which would grow as student numbers increase over the next decade. Obviously this is a somewhat theoretical calculation, since no such sudden transfer of resources is possible or desirable, but it points towards reforms that could be furthered with foreign assistance.

Meanwhile, foreign foundations could help quality publishers by funding more long-term programmes rather than single titles, as some do already. They could experiment with sales subsidies, paying publishers a percentage of the price of each book sold, but there would be resistance from publishers who would fear so much exposure to risk.

There is some criticism of Western foundations for creating unfair competition by favouring certain publishers, and for being interested primarily in promoting Western ideas rather than a more equal interchange that would also foster Hungarian writing. Foreign foundations may need to be more flexible and imaginative. “Sometimes,” said one publisher, “an air ticket can be more useful than a subsidy for a single title because it opens a contact or clinches a deal.”

Hungary also needs help not only with inward translations of Western authors but with outward translation and marketing of its own writings, fiction as well as non-fiction. At the moment there is little new Hungarian fiction but even domestically successful writers such as Peter Nadas have not been translated into English. One-way traffic discourages new talent and easily provokes fears of intellectual colonialism. CEEPP has understood this but some other donors have not.

Publishers would welcome loans at preferential rates in order to modernise, but so, doubtless, would other industries. Less controversial would be a better legal framework. Publishers still have too little protection against copyright theft and late payment by distributors, and the balance of rights is still tilted too far towards authors.

Quality publishing in Hungary is kept alive largely by the idealism of those who run it. Many are dedicated to culture for its own sake and some are driven by fears that Central Europe might again fall prey to illiberal ideas. Most will carry on as long as they can in adverse circumstances, earning little in the process, but there will inevitably be more failures over the next few years. "The trouble is," said one of older and more weary of them, "it is the only work we know. Some of us would love to move into the oil business."

## THE CZECH REPUBLIC

In the summer of 1994 students of Czech literature at Glasgow University were given a reading list of a couple of dozen Czech classics that they were to acquire on visits to the Czech Republic. They all returned empty handed. Not one of the books on the list was to be found in the bookshops of Prague or any other city.

This story from the late Igor Hajek, Senior Lecturer in Czech Studies at Glasgow University, helps to explain the worried debates among Prague intellectuals over the future of Czech culture. It seems at first difficult to reconcile with the crowded bookshops and streams of public visitors to the Prague Book Fair. But what were these people buying? Mostly reference books, technical books, business studies and foreign translations, when not relaxing with soft porn or popular fiction.

This is a new and disturbing situation for a country that has always prided itself on its cultural heritage. It follows an explosion of publishing that took place after the collapse of communism, when it seemed for a while that every good book ever written was dropping into the marketplace.

The explosion was more spectacular in Czechoslovakia than in neighbouring countries because the previous 20 years had been more oppressive. Whereas the communist regimes of Poland and Hungary had tolerated areas of independent thought, Prague's rulers lived in constant fear of the unquiet spirits of the Prague Spring of 1968. Protected by the Soviet occupation forces that installed them in 1969, they laid waste the cultural landscape. The best writers, thinkers, teachers and creative people were hounded into menial jobs or exile and in some cases imprisoned. Mediocrities were installed in their places, their loyalty bought with lavish subsidies for books, theatres, opera companies, orchestras, museums and films, all tightly censored. Prague alone had about two dozen theatres, and many provincial cities were generously supplied.

Such largesse by profoundly uncultured rulers was in the communist tradition, but early ideals of bringing culture to the masses had long since given way to more mundane hopes of buying up or buying off the intellectuals. The need to do this was particularly acute in Czechoslovakia because of the role intellectuals had played in the Prague Spring and further back in the nation's life. The regime therefore made sure that the rewards for loyalty and the penalties for opposition were substantial.

But it was not possible to maintain total control over all this creativity. Behind the scenes and in the grey areas around the edges of official culture, non-conformists could sometimes find space for coded messages of dissent, cautiously biting the hand that fed them, while banned writers occasionally slipped under the fence to write or translate under assumed names.

True freedom of expression, however, could be enjoyed only outside the perimeter of official culture by the intellectuals who had become window-cleaners, boilermen, construction workers and brewery hands (one of Vaclav Havel's jobs). These people, supported from abroad and published either abroad or in samizdat at home, kept alive the stubborn seeds of spiritual revival, which then sprouted as the regime weakened.

## Transition

After the revolution of November 1989, publishing took off. By the end of September 1990, 800 private publishers had joined the 36 owned by the state or state-approved organisations.[14] By early the following year the number had risen to anything between 1,500 or 4,000, depending on who was counting. Not all of them actually published books and some put out no more than one or two a year. This flowering represented a reaction to 20 years of repression and a return to an earlier tradition of small, semi-amateur publishers, of which there had been 1,400 before the communists took over in 1948.

New publications in this first exuberant wave were mainly works by formerly banned Czechoslovak writers, living and dead, and translations of similarly banned Western authors such as George Orwell. The public bought eagerly, and print runs of up to 100,000 were common. In 1990 Ivan Klima, who had been banned for many years, had five books published, all of which sold out immediately, some in runs of more than 100,000 copies.[15]

Large fortunes were made by those who seized the best opportunities, and the number of titles published rose sharply. Costs were low because paper and printing remained at old prices and most of the new publications were reprints of books that required no editing or serious marketing, and sometimes no payments for rights.

After such excitement, the coming down to earth was all the more painful. Paper and printing costs began to rise and the demand for previously forbidden works became saturated. Unsold books littered the shelves, and print runs dropped abruptly. In 1993 Ivan Klima's latest novel sold only 5,000 copies. "Where had all my readers gone?" he asked.[16]

By July 1992 publishers were starting to go bankrupt. Large publishers with heavy overheads such as Odeon and Albatros were the first to feel the pinch. All former state-owned publishers were hugely overstaffed, and the huge state-run printing presses were also inefficient. Odeon went into liquidation in November 1994, leaving its fine building to its main creditor, an Austrian bank. Avicenum, the state medical publisher, was another victim, although its medical programme has since been picked up by a successful private publisher, Grada, which established itself with translations of Western computer handbooks.

Small private publishers with lower overheads could do better, but often only by cutting corners, using cheap paper, and concentrating on reprints. Not all were champions of high culture. The dismissed communist Editor-in-Chief of a prestigious publishing house, Ceskoslovensky Spisovatel, went into business for himself and printed 87,000 copies of Kathleen Windsor's *Forever Amber*.

Soon small publishers were going bankrupt, and those that survived were in trouble. By 1993 the number of publishers putting out more than 10 titles a year had dropped to 500, although the number registered was still 2,683. The state distribution company Kniha, overloaded with unsold books, collapsed. Bookshops also closed, leaving some cities without a single one. By 1991 the national total had fallen from 1,800 to 500–700. In their place came a proliferation of street traders, often selling bankrupt stock acquired at large discounts through the Ministry of Culture, which had been criticised for storing these books in poor conditions.

Writers of all camps were dismayed by these first shocks of freedom. Some of the strongest complaints about the "soulless dictatorship of the marketplace" came from writers and artists of the old regime. But intellectuals who had been in opposition also accused Prime Minister Václav Klaus of destroying Czech culture. Already suspect among intellectuals for not having been in opposition, he was now described as a "Lenin of the Right" – a ruthless ideologue allegedly sacrificing the country's cultural soul for Utopian dreams of a pure market. Authors and publishers complained they were being treated as manufacturers, and their books as no different from saucepans. Their pleas for special status got short shrift. Klaus was quoted as saying "If you redecorate the house you move the library onto the balcony."[17] There was talk of abolishing the Ministry of Culture altogether, though this has now ceased, and the staff appears to have increased.

Battle was joined over Klaus's plan to tax literary and artistic activity at the same rate as other types of work, removing years of special privilege. There was also a struggle over VAT on books, which Klaus wanted to impose at the general rate of 23 per cent while authors and publishers fought for zero rating. Eventually the government, wanting to avoid all-out war with the writers, agreed to 5 per cent, which the publishing world still regards as excessive.

Views on Mr Klaus later mellowed somewhat as his economic policies seemed to be bearing fruit. Behind his smoke-screen of free market rhetoric he carefully cushioned the social effects of reform, kept prices and rents under control and protected vulnerable industries. He also accepted the principle, universally acknowledged throughout the democratic world, that culture must be subsidised, although not at the lavish level it enjoyed under socialism. More than a hundred institutions were accepted as worthy of subsidy – the national theatre, galleries, university libraries and some provincial theatres.

Books, however, were still in trouble. Funds diminished and readers' tastes changed. Interest in the coded, allusive works written by Czech writers under communism, and even those of Czech emigrés, diminished. Overall demand was expanding but in such a wide variety of directions that the market was transformed. After feasting on the forbidden fruits of the communist era, readers reached out for the huge variety of printed matter that had long been available to Western readers.

It was not so much the supposed Philistinism of Mr Klaus that now threatened Czech culture as the opening of the floodgates to international competition. Readers were discovering pornography, cheap romances, thrillers, popular history, books on self-development, psychology, feminism, the human body, how to get rich fast, and all the other essentials of Western life. Consumerism now seemed a more dangerous threat than censorship had ever been. Yet the list of best-sellers remained fairly eclectic, including, for instance, André Maurois' *History of England*, William Burroughs' *The Naked Lunch* and Lee Iacocca and Sonny Kleinfield's *Talking Straight*.

In other words, something like a normal book market was coming into being, hampered still by a weak legal structure, distorted prices, bad distribution and lack of buying power, but largely meeting the new demands of the majority of ordinary readers. A welcome sign of recovery was that the number of bookshops rose to its present level of more than 1,000. The cultural elite and the educational sector, however, remained deprived.

## Successes

As in the rest of the economy, some producers became rich while others were pushed to the wall. Smart operators were quick to seize the new opportunities. One such was Ivo Zelezny, head of the eponymous publishing house and probably Prague's most successful publisher, as well as being Vice-President of the Booksellers and Publishers Association and president of its Publishers Section. He started two weeks before the revolution of 1989 selling magazines through newspapers kiosks but lost all his capital and had to start again. In 1991 he published 40 titles, the following year 460, and the year after that 1,368. By the first quarter of 1994 he was already up to 357.

His innovation was to sell popular paperbacks through kiosks rather than bookshops, which had become uninterested in books that remained on the shelves more than a week or two. He prints his paperbacks in West Berlin because a printer there specialises in long, fast runs in standard sizes. His range includes P G. Wodehouse, Richard Gordon's comedies of life in the medical profession, and above all the Harlequin series of cheap romances. But he also publishes a few dozen serious books (a recent reference book on magic and a treatise on minorities, for instance), which put him among the top five quality publishers.

Even with his robust attitude to the marketplace, Dr Zelezny says that only half his books make a profit. "Overheads are still too high in relation to what Czech customers can afford, particularly with the high cost of foreign rights. We print for Western prices but sell in relation to our salaries – at about a tenth of the British prices. Theoretically it is impossible to publish here but for many people it is a hobby or they get support," he says.

He is big enough to deal directly with booksellers but he complains that they often buy only five copies of a book and do not re-order. They only want quick turnover. The cost of sending one book to a bookshop is very high because of postage and bank transfers. In addition, the high cost of storage discourages stocking. He has had books returned to his warehouse by a distributor, even after they were paid for, because the cost of storage was too high.

His list of complaints about government policy is much the same as that of more specialist publishers. He had to send 23 free copies of each book to libraries, even paying postage, which can be a third of the price of a book. From July 1995 the number will be reduced to four, which is welcomed by publishers but not by libraries. He would like lower postage rates for books, zero VAT, and legislation to speed up payments and make it possible, as in Germany, to write off non-paid debts as losses for tax purposes.

A rather different type of success has been enjoyed by Alexander Tomsky, Director of Academia, the publishing house of the Czech Academy of Sciences. He learned publishing in exile in London and then with his own Rozmluvy Press in Prague. Within 12 months of taking over Academia in January 1993 he turned a loss of about $350,000 into modest profit of $5,800.[18]

He fizzes with enthusiasm. "The market is marvellous now," he says. "People are thrilled by books and talk about them. In real terms book prices have gone down. The market is still growing. I can make a profit on runs of 5,000."

But he admits he gains a big advantage from being owned by the Academy. "I pay no rent for huge offices in Wenceslas Square, a bookshop, a huge warehouse and my own vans, so I am in unfair competition with the private sector. Eventually this will be unacceptable because subsidies to academies are being cut and buildings can be sold for millions. But for now, my overheads are nil."

Academia has two sections, one sponsored by the Academy, the other commercial. Sponsored books mostly sell no more than 600–1,000 copies. The commercial side publishes about 30 titles a year and has put out a wide variety of works, including *Rules of Czech*

*Orthography* with a print run of 45,000; an English–Czech dictionary (50,000); *Quasi-blasphemous Songs and Poems* by Karel Kryl (38,000), which sold out very quickly on the strength of the author's broadcasts on Radio Free Europe; and Paul Johnson's *History of the Twentieth Century* (30,000).

However, he too has his complaints. Authors do not understand that publishers also have rights, he says. Under communism, publishers simply provided workshops that printed to order. Now they are entrepreneurs who take risks. "This is an unknown concept. If an author gets excerpts published in a paper because he knows an editor, he wants the royalties for himself; the publisher is left out. The author argues that if he had not written this work of genius nobody could make anything. But a publisher may publish 50 books a year and make a profit on only five, so if he hits the jackpot it has to pay for all the others. I am risking large sums of money all the time, knowing that only a few will succeed. The copyright law must be sorted out. It is too much in favour of the authors."

Although others disagree, he insists that prices could be raised without losing buyers. Often it is poorer people who buy books because they cannot afford larger luxuries such as cars. Distribution is also very bad, says. Wholesalers are fragmented and lack computers and capital, which also reduces potential profits.

Also helped by rent-free premises is Dr Vladimir Pistorius, Director of Mlada Fronta, which publishes about 100 titles a year with 40 employees, of whom a quarter work in sales. The day of the amateur is over, he says. Now is the time for professionalism. He learnt a lot at a course at Stanford University: "That kind of foreign help is the most useful." He says that nearly half the price of a book is accounted for by production, compared with about 15 per cent in Britain.

He, too, complains about distribution. He deals directly with booksellers, including 150 in Prague, but booksellers pay late and courts work very slowly. It can take a year to recover a debt, by which time the creditor may be bankrupt too. A better distribution system would reduce overheads but not necessarily increase demand. One problem is that postal charges make it expensive to send out promotional material, so there is not enough information on books available.

Good translations of fiction are particularly difficult to publish because of high copyright fees and lack of time to check and read. They are much more expensive to produce than domestic fiction. There is too little foreign help for fiction, he says. Fiction, he emphasises, makes an important contribution to culture, education, social development and international contacts.

These success stories are offered as examples of how it is possible to make money as a publisher either by plunging into outright commercialism or with the help of free assets held over from the old system. Even publishers with these advantages, however, find it difficult to cope with the discrepancy between high production costs and low retail prices.

## Struggle for support

Serious publishers without their advantages and lacking the taste or the skills for commercialism have a much more difficult time. Publishing is still a partly amateur industry with many individuals working from home or employing minimal assistance. Those who survive as serious enterprises do so largely by mastering the time-consuming skills of applying for subsidies.

One of the most appealing examples in this sector is Torst, run with verve and dedication by Viktor Stoilov and Jan Sulc. At the 1994 Prague Book Fair their imaginative stand, with its classical columns and gilt chairs, stood out from the plastic cubicles of other publishers. Torst has managed to create a brand image that attracts a core of 2–3,000 loyal readers confident that anything it publishes must be worth reading. It sold 11,000 copies of the memoirs of Anastaz Opasek, a popular priest and television personality who has a following among young people. It also publishes books on poetry, modern literature, works by Witold Gombrowicz, Czeslaw Milosz and Elias Canetti, for instance.

But Stoilov and Sulc have to dedicate a lot of their time to applying for help from foreign foundations. They have other problems too. Distribution is especially difficult for small publishers. Booksellers outside Prague often cannot get Torst's books, or do not find it worth ordering single copies because the cost of postage and bank transfers is higher than the bookseller's margin. Sending catalogues and literature by post is also too expensive. And even when bookshops order they pay the distributor very late, so the distributor delays payment to the publisher, who then has to carry the burden of credit at high interest rates.

Another small quality publisher is Prostor, which puts out about 6–10 books a year on politics, psychology and related matters, as well as some poetry and fiction. It aims to publish a mix of profitable and non-profitable books but it is not really interested in commercial publishing. It has published work by George Soros, Karl Popper and Jacques Rupnik. For the foreseeable future, says Prostor's Director, Ales Lederer, he will need financial help to pay for foreign copyright and translations. Even then some are out of reach. He was quoted £300,000 for the rights to Margaret Thatcher's memoirs.

Prostor also publishes a journal of ideas whose circulation has dropped from 12,000 in 1990 to around 2,000 in 1994. Lederer says the decline is the result of a change in the social atmosphere and the decline of interest in the communist period. Readers are distracted by the flood of other journals and magazines, and bookshops will not buy the journal because demand is too low. Selling by direct subscription, which accounts for 20 per cent of circulation, is not satisfactory because the postal system is slow, unreliable and expensive, making subscription copies more expensive than shop copies – the opposite of usual practice in the West.

## Academic publishing

Academic publishing requires urgent attention because of the long-term implications for the generation now going through the educational system. The shortage of funds is acute. Teachers and students at school and university levels cannot get the books they need. University and public libraries are very underfunded. There is still a huge need for basic Western works on sciences and some of the narrower specialities. Economics, law and management are better served because the demand is high and American publishers in these fields are swift to hire local translators.

Small academic publishers of journals and books have a difficult time because there is so little money in the academic world. Students and teachers are poor, and libraries and research institutions are under-funded. There is a shortage even of basic reference works, dictionaries, encyclopedias and grammar books.

One small publisher that struggles in the academic world is SLON, run by Alena Miltova. It concentrates on sociology, which has suffered 20 years of isolation from the West, having had to get all its books from the Soviet Union, East Germany and Poland. SLON has to sell most of its books at about half the cost price. Since 1991 it has published 15 books and planned another seven for 1994. It is commissioning a series of textbooks by holding a competition among potential authors in cooperation with the department of sociology in Brno, finding it cheaper to commission works by domestic authors, who can draw on world literature, than to translate and buy rights for original foreign works.

SLON also publishes a quarterly journal of sociology that started as a samizdat publication under communism. Unlike more academic journals it offers essays of general interest, literary analysis, and information on developments abroad, attracting readers far outside academic sociology. But it survives only with foreign help and because it can call on volunteer labour and administrative support from the sociology faculty.

There is much discussion about how best to help students, says Miltova. Might there be special grants to authors of textbooks, or a system of book vouchers or subsidised bookshop credits to help students buy more books? A related debate is over whether to admit all qualified students to university and weed them out later, putting a heavy burden on resources, or to select by competitive exam so as to keep numbers down. And should accommodation be subsidised, or the students themselves? On the answers to these questions will depend, in part, the health of the academic book trade.

Whatever happens, foreign help will remain important to the academic sector, particularly for foreign rights and translations, although these costs are likely to diminish as rising generations learn to read English fluently. Meanwhile, as elsewhere in Central Europe, there is heavy reliance on *scripta*, the bound sheets of lecture notes. Charles University produced 197 *scripta* titles in 1993 but is now re-examining them in the light of criticism that they are of uneven quality and discourage the circulation of ideas among different universities.

## Distribution

The entire book trade suffers from a ragged distribution system that is both inefficient and far too expensive in relation to the cost of books. Publishers are unwilling or unable to cooperate and distrust the idea of going back to centralised distribution. The high cost of storage discourages stocking. Small booksellers outside Prague find it too expensive to order small quantities of books, and are not interested in those that will not sell fast. Many are unskilled, and they work on small margins against rents that are rising to Western levels or beyond, especially in central Prague. Some larger publishers deal directly with booksellers while others rely on a jumble of some 15 distributors, of whom only two or three cover the whole country.

So far no computer network links bookshops to publishers and wholesalers. This gap may be filled by a firm called Albertina Icome of Prague which is developing a CD-ROM bibliography of Czech books published since 1983, with more than 84,000 titles, and adding 8,000 every year.

## Funding

Czech publishing is still a long way from being able to operate without subsidies. The Ministry of Culture has 2.5 million crowns a year to support domestic publishing in any language but not translations. Dr Zeleny reckons that this sum can cover losses on about 25 books published in 1,000 copies and sold for prices slightly above the average retail price. In reality the subsidy usually covers about a quarter of the losses on each book. Next year, the government will introduce special awards to support foreign translations of Czech writers.

Up to now, funds have been disbursed on the recommendation of a committee appointed by the Minister of Culture. This has been regarded as wrong in principle but reasonably effective in practice for as long as the Ministry remains in safe hands. In the first nine months of 1994, 113 applications were received, of which 57 were approved. A new draft law expected to be passed in 1995 will hand responsibility to the book section of a new independent Arts Council over which the Minister will have only a formal veto.

The present committee is chaired by Ivan Klima and meets four times a year. Initially, its members, several of whom are authors or publishers, were barred only from voting on their own requests for subsidies. Then it was realised that members with their own bids in would be tempted to vote down other requests in the hope of leaving more money for themselves, so the new rules forbid any member who has put in an application to vote on any subsidy.

The committee tries to assess not only quality but also the marketability of the work and the business aspects of proposals. It decided, for instance, that the memoirs of a decadent poet of the last century would be of such limited appeal that it would be better photocopied. Members receive no remuneration for what probably amounts to a total of about two weeks' work a year, according to Klima. A similar committee was set up in 1994 to help magazines and journals.

Limited funds are also available from the Writers' Guild, founded after 1989 as successor to the Writers' Union, which was dissolved in the early 1970s and replaced by a new one, which lasted until 1989. It is open to everyone but the younger generation tends to stay away, so most active members are over 60.

The Guild has been able to set up a capital fund administered by a committee from which it makes grants to publishers of living authors, including promising beginners. Usually it reckons to cover only printing costs, which make up about 60 per cent of total costs. For instance, it supported publication by Torst of the diary of the poet Jan Zabrana, expecting it to lose money. Instead, it was unexpectedly successful but the Guild did not get its money back. It could presumably stretch its funds further by making loans that are repaid when a book is successful but written off when not, as the Stefan Batory Foundation does in Poland.

## Philanthropy

A potential domestic source of funds is private business, which occasionally helps publishing. The Ceska Pojistovna insurance company, for instance, supported the publication of Marie Sulcova's *Polocas nadeji*. But at such an early stage in the development of the free market there is little spare capital around, and only limited interest in donating what there is to culture, except for prestigious events such as opera, concerts or exhibitions. The country may have strong cultural traditions but its history has been shaped just as much by stolid, bourgeois materialism.

More may be available from private and business donors when there is a law in place on non-profit organisations. A new draft law has been held up by the Prime Minister, who distrusts intellectuals and dislikes tax loopholes, fearing they will be exploited for private gain. He is probably right. Since 1989 more than 20,000 organisations have registered as non-profit but their ill-defined legal status has enabled some people to exploit them for tax avoidance. As Pavel Tigrid, Minister of Culture, points out, the culture surrounding non-profit organisations in the West is unfamiliar in today's Central Europe. It is difficult to find people enjoying sufficient public trust to administer such funds for the general good. There is no elite of "the great and the good", nor a solid foundation of middle class civic morality.

Nevertheless, strong pressure has been exerted on Klaus to take the non-profit sector more seriously for the contribution it can make to civil society, and the business world, led by the Commercial Bank in Prague, recently took steps of its own by setting up a Cultural Fund of Entrepreneurs.

Most of the smaller and more serious publishers remain heavily dependent on foreign sources and devote a great deal of time to tapping them. Some governments, mainly the French, German, Austrian and Swiss, finance translations of their own literature into Czech. Germany has provided funds over two years for translating German works into Czech but it is sometimes accused of presenting a "folkloristic" picture of German culture. Britain and Scandinavia do little or nothing at government level to finance outward translation of their own books. More helpful are foundations, particularly the German political foundations, the Robert Bosch Foundation and the Mellon Foundation, which is funding a computerised bibliography for the National Library.

Opinions vary on what would happen if foreign funds were withdrawn or seriously diminished. A few writers and publishers take the robust view that the people who moan about the demise of Czech culture are mediocrities who cannot get published because they are not good enough. Most experts, however, feel that such a small market as that of the Czech Republic will always need special help if it is not to be swamped by foreign products and taken over by foreign companies. This help should, however, gradually come more from domestic sources. Pistorius says that only small amounts would be sufficient to keep Czech publishing healthy, maybe 15 million crowns a year. For comparison, theatres receive about 300 million a year from the state.

There is fairly widespread agreement that a good manuscript will always find a publisher, although it may still need financial help, but good new writing is still in short supply. As the older writers from the communist period lose their domestic audience, new writers are only starting to find their feet. There are some promising people amongst them, such as Jachym Topol and Michal Viewegh, who should eventually make their mark. Ivan Klima says that he does not know of a single book worth printing that cannot be published in the Czech Republic. If new authors are good enough to reach international audiences foreign publishers would expect to take them up on a normal commercial basis.

Even for an established writer, however, it is virtually impossible to make a full-time living from the Czech market alone. Occasional exceptions can be found in the area of popular fiction. One such is Vladimir Paral, a former chemical engineer who managed to write on the social scene in the 1970s–80s without mentioning the party. Now a stalwart of the New Erotic Initiative, a club that features scantily clad waitresses, his most recent book is *Playgirls I*. Also successful is Zdena Frybova, who writes sensational novels about the contemporary scene.

More serious writers have to rely on other jobs or foreign earnings. Ivan Klima says that his total earnings from Czech sales of his last book were less than he was paid for one article in *Der Spiegel*. His main earnings come from foreign sales. Many writers, as in the West, rely on teaching, journalism and television work to provide their main incomes, but the decline in the film industry and the import of foreign television programmes may shrink this type of support for aspiring writers.

## Danger of isolation

Jiri Grusa, former opposition writer and translator, now ambassador to Bonn, says the main danger is that the Czech Republic will become provincialized and intellectually isolated if it is not helped to remain in the European mainstream. Just as industrial products must be competitive in world markets, so must culture if it is to thrive, he argues. Internationalism is particularly important if narrow nationalism is to be discouraged. For this Czech culture needs, and will continue to need, supplementary funds for foreign rights, translations, both inward and outward, and to support foreign exchanges in the cultural and academic worlds. There is a lot of ground to make up, he points out, because philosophy and the humanities were badly neglected under communism.

Grusa and Pistorius also point out that too little is being done to foster cultural and academic contacts within the countries of the former Warsaw Pact. Among the Visegrad Four, some of the old dissident contacts have survived, but generally there is far too little interchange. If

Western aid-givers do not recognise this, their help could contribute to creating an unhealthy situation in which all the cultural connections in the area are with the West and not with each other.

## Conclusions

The worst of the post-revolutionary turmoil is over. The publishing industry is gradually coming to terms with the new conditions, and rival publishers' unions have merged. A new copyright law is in preparation. Something like a "normal" market is coming into being. One can almost envy the excitement of Czech readers at joining the rest of the world after so many years of isolation. Ivan Klima even goes so far as to assert that "Czech culture, for all its difficulties, is more in a renaissance than in a dark age."[19]

Nevertheless, it would be wrong to be too complacent about the situation. Small publishers are struggling to meet demand for serious books, and are particularly reluctant to publish Czech writers because they cannot afford to take risks. Their problems are now worsening because of recent sharp increases in the price of paper. By March 1995 it will have risen by up to 80 per cent over the previous twelve months. This will add 50 per cent to the costs of books with short print runs and is expected to put many small publishers out of business, together with some larger ones, too.

More investment in educational publishing in particular is urgently needed if rising generations are not to suffer lasting deprivation. It would be worth considering subsidies specifically for university bookshops. The government also needs to think more seriously about tax concessions for books, reduced postage rates, payment for compulsory deliveries to libraries (even though these have been reduced), legislation against late payments and modification of the present imposition of VAT on gifts from abroad. Some gifts of computers have had to be returned because the recipient could not afford the 25 per cent tax. Libraries have even had to pay VAT on the return of books they have lent abroad, and authors have been asked to pay VAT on their own free copies from foreign publishers. This is absurd.

Foreign funding still has an important role to play in helping with translations and rights for foreign books. For the broadest effect, however, help should be going – as some already is – into the modernisation of distribution systems and libraries, both university and public. With so many new titles on the market, customers need more help in selecting from what is available. The information revolution will eventually come to their aid, particularly in schools and universities. It should also facilitate a more consistent supply of books for which demand is low, since reprinting will become quicker and cheaper. For the time being, however, there is a good case for propping up some of the small quality publishers who keep faith with Czech culture. It is symptomatic of the strains on Czech publishing that Bertelsmann is starting to put a few Czech classics on the shelves.

## SLOVAKIA

"Tunnels, not bridges," said a young Slovak publisher, putting me right on his links with the Czech intelligentsia. In reality, secrecy seems neither necessary nor practised in the dense network of contacts that survive between Slovak and Czech intellectuals, but he was speaking a few days after the formation of Vladimir Meciar's second government in December 1994, when clouds of foreboding were descending over the liberal intelligentsia.

The most anti-liberal forces in the country were coming together in his red-brown coalition of former communists, radical nationalists and his own Movement for a Democratic Slovakia. The new Minister of Education was Eva Slavkovská, of the Slovak National Party, notorious for her anti-Hungarian sentiments and her promise to impose Slovak language schools in Hungarian areas. Privatisation was put in the hands of Peter Bisak of the left-wing Slovak Workers Association, which has opposed privatisation in principle and vowed to press for a new system giving the government more control over whose hands reach the honey pot. His party has also been against membership of the European Union.

Even without this new threat, the clandestine mentality seems more difficult to shake off in Slovakia than in the other Visegrad countries. The shadows of the past hang heavier here, and change has been slow. Slovakia is more isolated from the West than the Czech lands, more conservative, more dependent on heavy industry, less favoured by foreign investment and readier to accept negative stereotypes of the West. Its image of itself is confused, deeply imbued with xenophobia and the mythology of a thousand years of oppression.[20]

The roots of anti-liberal thinking go back to the last century, fed by a complex combination of Russian authoritarianism, Hungarian bureaucracy, Roman Catholic fundamentalism and rural traditions forcibly dragged into heavy industrialisation by the communists. Opposition before 1989 was more limited than in the Czech lands, although it eventually brought together a loose alliance of independent Catholics, environmentalists, liberal writers, artists and scientists.

Since 1989 the political apparatus has resisted reform (except when it can make money from privatisation) and so has the population. A survey in October 1993 found that fewer than 20 per cent supported liberal ideas and 89 per cent believed the state should guarantee jobs for everyone.[21] After the split in January 1993, reforms were delayed by the first government of Vladimir Meciar, then briefly pushed forward by Jozef Moravcik after Meciar's fall in March 1994, only to be slowed down again with return of Meciar after elections in October 1994, when all the direct privatisations approved since 6 September were annulled.

## Government support

Government support for books is administered by a body called Pro Slovakia. Supposedly independent, it is in fact subject to government policy. Meciar changes its board whenever he is in power, and the Minister of Culture can – and does – veto its decisions. It consists of a council with 13 committees covering all aspects of culture, including art, music, theatre, monuments and books. There are two committees for books. One, which disbursed 6 million crowns in 1994, is for belles lettres, history and related subjects. The other spent 2.2 million crowns on scientific books. Only Slovak books qualify for support, and about one application in ten is approved.

There is another fund with about 17 million crowns to support books and magazines for young people, and there are plans to provide money for translating Slovak authors into foreign languages. A further 7 million is available from another department for minorities, including Hungarians, Ukrainians, gypsies and Russians.

About 3,500 new titles were published in 1994 but runs were generally much lower than in the past. All Slovak books must register with ISBN and pay 6 per cent VAT, a low rate that is also applied to food, while other goods are charged at 25 per cent. There are no concessionary postal rates for books although the Ministry of Culture shows a lively interest in the idea. Writers have to pay 2 per cent of their earnings into the Literary Fund, which assists writers and translations.

## Education

Slovak publishing suffers heavily from the lack of money devoted to education, made worse by the rise in the number of students (from 49,154 in 1989/90 to 55,564 in 1992/3) and the need for new types of course.[22] Under the first Meciar government, education was squeezed in an effort to meet the pressure from international lending institutions to cut the budget deficit. In 1993 spending on higher education fell sharply and the Slovak Rectors' Conference warned the government that the higher education system was experiencing an "intellectual collapse" and that standards could not be maintained in costly fields such as medicine and science.[23]

According to Juraj Svec, Rector of Comenius University, 936 employees, representing about 20 per cent of the teaching staff, left in 1993. Large numbers are also working abroad because of the lack of equipment at home. By 1994 only 2.3 per cent of GDP was being spent on science and technology. At the same time the break-up of Czechoslovakia was depriving Slovakia of valuable interchange with Czech universities.

Lubomir Harach, the previous Minister of Education, sought a 25 per cent increase in spending on education. The new minister is expected to be much less sympathetic and more likely to waste money on nationalist projects. Further cuts in education seem likely. The outlook for the educational system and the publishers who supply it is therefore gloomy.[24]

## The intelligentsia

In this retrograde atmosphere, former dissidents retain the sense of purpose in their struggle for liberal values, and some even suspect that the secret police have not entirely lost interest in them. "The situation is clearer here than in the Czech Republic, and the lines are more sharply drawn," says a former underground publisher in Bratislava. "Czech intellectuals are afraid to criticise Klaus's government for fear of being accused of leftism. Here the government is rubbish and manipulates the media while independent publications oppose it, so we know where we are."

The intellectual community is deeply polarised, and the writers' organisations have fragmented. One group includes right-wing nationalists and former servants of the communist regime who now largely support the government. Its chairman, Jan Tuzinsky, is a member of parliament for Meciar's party and also Director of Radio. Their journals are *Literarny Tyzdennik* and *Slovenske pohl'ady*, both in receipt of government funds, direct or indirect, and the group also has a new publishing house. The other main group brings together six organisations representing a wider spectrum including liberals and Hungarians, while a smaller group has also recently emerged between the two.

The urban intelligentsia were mostly against the break-up of Czechoslovakia, and they still consciously foster relations with Prague. Hence the talk of tunnels and bridges. They are haunted by the feeling of being the poor relation of Prague, culturally as well as economically, and they worry that efforts to promote a specifically Slovak culture can too easily be mistaken for nationalism. Many foreign books have never been translated into Slovak because the Slovak intelligentsia can read

Czech as easily as their own language. Czechs can also read Slovak, though less easily as they have had less practice, so the cultural frontier is blurred.

## Small independents

A frontier is, however, gradually forming. Even liberal Slovak intellectuals realise that if Slovakia is to establish its identity it must consciously develop its own language. "We cannot rely on reading in Czech or the original because our language needs to evolve to express new ideas," says Martin Simecka, a former underground publisher who is now Director of Archa. This is a small but vigorous publishing house, unique in its exclusive dedication to the humanities, mainly philosophy, sociology, aesthetics and history. "Translations are vital for the development of language. This is why basic books, especially in philosophy, must be translated into Slovak as well as Czech," he argues.

Disentangling the publishing worlds of the two countries is a slow process. Many publishers on both sides of the frontier cultivate both markets. Even Archa sells about a third of its production to the Czech Republic and struggles with the problems of duplication. It has sometimes negotiated for translation rights and then found that a Czech publisher has got there first and is already marketing the book in Slovakia. Recently it had to stop publication of a big book on religion because a Czech translation appeared first, wasting the time of its Slovak translator. Now Archa, like other Slovak publishers, tries to buy Czech rights at the same time, even if only to hold them for a year or so.

Simecka is the son of the late Milan Simecka, a well-known philosopher and opposition writer under communism whose name is now attached to a foundation that promotes democracy, civic culture and improved relations between the Czech and Slovak nations. Archa pursues broadly the same aims. Its main purposes, according to its brochure, "is to fill in the tremendous gap in the education of an entire society, which was spiritually devastated for 40 years by an ideological regime, to help understand the way of thinking which has formed contemporary Europe and America. We believe that by publishing exceptional books we are helping to create a place for the spiritual development of the intellectual community, which is the basis for development towards an open society in Slovakia."

Archa's list includes Foucault, Derrida, Isaiah Berlin, Dworkin, Giovanni Sartori, Raymond Aron, Roger Scruton, Emmanuel Kant and Ralf Dahrendorf, plus new Slovak novelists such as Jana Juranova and Alta Vasova. "We decide what is important, not what is popular," says Simecka. Typical runs for books of philosophy are 1–4,000. He has made a point of filling in the blank spots in Slovakia's history with books on the deportation of Jews, the persecution of the Catholic Church and the "almost unknown political life in Slovakia" from 1860 to 1989. He has published the documents of the Charter 77 movement and a collection of UN documents on human rights, and was the first to publish Vaclav Havel's essays in Slovak. He is trying to fill gaps in scientific literature, particularly in new areas such as artificial intelligence, cosmology and genetics. He is also, thanks partly to CEEPP's help, the Slovak representative in the vast pan-European project called *The Making of Europe*, a multi-volume series in at least five languages, intended to challenge national histories with a European perspective on the continent's evolution.

The universities are Archa's main target, and it draws on academic expertise for the preparation of many of its books. It is producing a series of books for students costing 20–30 crowns. About 60 per cent of the costs are covered by assistance because the "real" price is about 100 crowns and no student could pay that. Reprints are a particular problem because a run of 1,000 copies is necessary for it to be worthwhile.

Simecka says that only a handful of Slovak publishers are interested in serious books and even they bring out very few, whereas several successful Czech publishers publish loss-making intellectual books to improve their image. Archa is therefore unique in Slovakia. It could not survive without foreign support for individual titles or series, but this is not easy to find. "I spend half my time looking for sponsors," says Simecka. "It's a nightmare. The closing of CEEPP is a serious problem. If we could sell books for 200 crowns we could survive without help."

Foreign foundations show little interest in Slovak authors, he adds, suspecting that some of them may be reluctant to alienate business interests by supporting controversial authors. Archa, he says, is "the cuckoo's egg in Slovak culture."

Guaranteed purchases are a useful form of help. Archa is preparing four books on law with the help of the best lawyers and hopes that the journalists' organisation will buy the one on press law for its 2,000 members. Editions of human rights documents have been bought by the Milan Simecka foundation for distribution at its workshops.

The USIA is "useless" in his view because it has a very limited view of suitable books. The Germans and the French also tend to suggest titles of their own, and the Germans are "too bureaucratic". Archa recently published five German authors but received German support for only one. Jewish organisations have been reluctant to finance Jewish memoirs of the Second World War, and so far no one has a offered assistance for the memoirs of President Masaryk's secretary, a Slovak woman with an outsider's inside view of the first Czechoslovak government.

Archa also lacks money for promotion, relying largely on friends to mention or review its books. It usually gives more than a hundred free copies to newspapers and journals, plus the obligatory 15 copies to state institutions. "We are probably the most reviewed publishing house in Slovakia," says Simecka. Frequently, however, reviews do not help to sell books, partly because of the poverty of the intelligentsia. TV advertising is too expensive, and TV book programmes are a "dirty business".

## Distribution

Closely linked to Archa by ties of friendship, former opposition activity and common interest in serious books is Art Forum, a small distributor with two shops in Bratislava and one in Kosice. "We could not survive without Art Forum although they owe us a lot of money," says Simecka.

Art Forum's origins go back to the dissident Czechoslovak Jazz Section of the 1980s, and the link is still audible in its main shop, where customers browse among heavy books on philosophy to a somewhat incongruous (to Western ears) background of modern rock or jazz. After 1989, Art Forum found that the Jazz Section had "accounting problems" so it broke away and registered separately as a limited company in 1990. The initial idea was a club, says Vlado Michal, one of the founders, where young people and students would come to read books and listen to music. Now the young have less money so its profile its changing, although the music survives.

Yet Art Forum still sells mainly to intellectuals and students, who, in spite of their poverty, are often forced to buy because libraries do not have sufficient copies of standard works. Good sellers have been Hans Joachim Störing's *History of Philosophy* in Czech and Paul Johnson's *History of the Twentieth Century* published by Rozmluvy in Prague.

Its underground origins have not wholly vanished, nor have its connections with the Czech intelligentsia. Indeed, it owes its position in the market partly to the fact that it was able to continue supplying Czech books after the split, when Czech books suddenly became foreign imports. Its bookshop in Kosice relies heavily on Czechs who came there to work at the big steel mill. It was opened in response to a large number of mail orders from around 300 regular customers in that city, among them a now almost legendary figure, a Czech engineer and former samizdat reader who was ordering about 15 books a month. In its brief existence the shop has become a magnet for critical intellectuals and is regarded as the place to make contact with the opposition. Kosice also happens to be the home of *Domino efekt*, a vigorous critical journal that is "against everything", according to one of its happy readers.

In spite of its important niche in the quality market, and as a supplier of Czech books, Art Forum lives on the edge of survival. Apart from a little help from the Open Society Fund to publish two art books, its only outside assistance comes in the form of tolerance by friendly publishers, particularly Archa, who put up with being paid late. "We transfer our economic problems to publishers," admits Michal. "They suffer with us by agreeing – mostly – to late payment, which helps our cash flow." A stronger law on prompt payments, for which many publishers yearn, would create more problems than it would solve for an enterprise of this sort.

With books still relatively cheap, the percentage on each sale is low. Art Forum is both a distributor and retailer so it earns most when it sells directly from its shops. "If we buy a book for 70 crowns, we sell it in the shop for 100 crowns, but if we sell on to other shops we keep only 7 per cent and the shop gets 20–25 per cent."

Art Forum's greatest need is for capital, preferably cheaper than at the going rate of 18 per cent. It needs vans for distribution and computers for cataloguing, stock-keeping and accounting. It cannot raise bank loans because its stock of books is not regarded as a capital asset and its premises are rented. Nor can it get loans from the European Union's PHARE programme, which is supposed to help small businesses. It was able to open the new branch in Kosice only by transferring stock from another shop in Bratislava, but fortunately the risk has paid off.

## Large publishers

At the opposite end of the scale is Slovensky spisovatel', the largest publisher of fiction and poetry in Bratislava, which brings out about 90 books a year. Founded in 1951 as a state firm dedicated to contemporary literature, it has been a limited company since 1 January 1993. It now tries to sustain the same role with the addition of foreign bestsellers such as Dick Francis, Frederick Forsyth, Daphne du Maurier and Danielle Steel, all of whose works make a profit. It also expects to do well with Julian Barnes's *History of the World in 10 1/2 Chapters*, and is publishing Tolkien's *The Hobbit* without outside funding.

Nonetheless, it finds life in the marketplace far from easy. When it has paid for expensive foreign rights it needs a run of at least 50,000 to break even, so it targets the Czech Republic too. It suffers the familiar problems of high costs, low prices, complex distribution systems and late payment from wholesalers and bookshops, who are often "not very honest partners," complains Martin Chovanec, Chairman and Managing Director. Partly for this reason he has formed a book club, which supplies outlying areas by post, cash on delivery.

Like some of the large Polish publishers, Chovanec is unhappy about the difficulty of negotiating directly with American publishers, who prefer to work through agents such as the controversial Gerd Plessl, now with an office in Bratislava. "American publishers are interested only in business, and have no time for publishers from small countries," he complains. British and European publishers, he says, are more willing to cooperate directly and are more flexible. (His remarks apply mainly to trade publishers, since many academic and educational publishers have long worked directly with publishers in the region.)

Training courses such as those provided in Slovakia by International Book Development of London were very useful in the early days of transition, says Chovanec, when it was necessary to learn about the basics of commercial publishing, company structures, boards of directors, shares, and so on, but this type of help is no longer necessary. It takes too much time, and visiting instructors often do not know enough about the environment. (For a different view see more on this subject under *Training* in the concluding section.)

Slovak publishers can learn much more when they are attached to Western publishers and can observe them operating in their own environment, select what to apply at home and above all make contacts. In fact, says Chovanec, the Slovak edition of *The Hobbit* is the result of his spending three days with HarperCollins and attending the London Book Fair. He was also grateful for a subsidy from the British Publishers Association to attend an International Rights Seminar. More help for travelling, attending seminars and making contacts with Western publishers would be extremely useful, especially as accommodation is very expensive in London and Prague.

He is amused but sometimes pained by Western ignorance of his country and, like many of his colleagues, would like to be taken more seriously. "We are not a strange, backward country. We want to meet managers at the same level. We want to be treated like normal colleagues, not strange creatures from another world." Slovakia, he points out, suffers from not having had well-known emigrés and dissidents like the Czechs to make its literature known abroad.

Slovensky spisovatel' seeks support for many of its books but has difficulty finding help for fiction. The most helpful countries are the smaller ones such as Israel, Denmark, Holland and the Scandinavian states because they want to promote their literature. The French have supported editions of Camus, Sartre, George Perec and other French authors. English-speaking countries are generally less generous. Twenty-five titles by Slovak writers were supported by the government fund Pro Slovakia, which paid a percentage of the budget. But even a relatively popular Slovak writers such as Hana Zelinova sells only 4–5,000 copies and makes no profit.

The main public demand is for books from the English-speaking world, although writers with Russian-sounding names such as Asimov and Doctorow evoke confusion and are not popular. Clare Frances is popular when she is not describing her experiences on the Russian border, "which we know too much about." Books on China are uninteresting because "your experience is different from ours." Thrillers get a mixed reception because "people don't want fear – they know it already. They want to feel good." Even in the quest for good feelings, however, there are some depths to which Slovensky spisovatel' will not sink. Barbara Cartland is "below the bottom level, fiction for servants".

Another large state house, Tatran, is in a far worse state, reportedly tottering on the brink of collapse and heavily in debt. Rumours circulate that some of its managers are using the facilities to run private firms, maybe hoping to buy it cheap. Another rumour is that Meciar is about to present it to one of his friends under the new arrangements for privatisation. His government is more hostile to foreign partners than was the previous government.

Stefan Grena, Editor-in-Chief, will discuss none of this but admits that the firm is in limbo at present. It was privatised in March 1994 but the decision was cancelled after the October election. Now it waits, unable to plan, or even publish. It published 120 titles in 1990, 80 in 1992, 60 in 1993, and 10 between January and April 1994. Since then none.

"We have manuscripts prepared," says Grena, "but we dare not risk going ahead because the new owners might refuse to pay the printers or honour rights contracts." Although nominally state-owned, Tatran receives no subsidy. Its only income now comes from renting out offices to private companies in its elegant premises in the centre of town – a valuable capital asset that attracts many covetous eyes.

Tatran was once a distinguished state publishing house specialising in classical literature, both Slovak and international, especially fiction, art books and children's books. A former employee described how it used to be. "We published Plato, Plutarch, Cicero, Pushkin, Lermontov and Flaubert very cheaply – 110 crowns for three volumes of Flaubert and we sold 13,500 copies, 75 crowns for two volumes of Cicero. Before 1989 there was an almost guaranteed market of up to 10,000 members of the intelligentsia. In 1992 we could still sell 5,000 copies of André Gide but not now. No one has time or money. Everyone has to work so hard they can't read heavy books any more, even if they can afford them. People want happy endings, lighter stuff. I myself, now running a publishing house of my own, am often too tired to read much. In the old days I could spend months editing a book, hours agonizing over one sentence and then read all evening. Not any longer. We did not know how lucky we were. Those days have gone for ever. But I would not want them back for all the other reasons."

Today, says Grena, the public simply do not buy as many books as they once did, or anyway not serious books, since prices are 2–4 times what they were in 1989 and most incomes have fallen. Things were particularly difficult after the split with the Czech Republic because Slovakia was so little known abroad and all the foreign help had been going to Prague. Moreover, Czech books had been circulating freely and meeting much of the demand. The French were the most helpful because they always make a determined effort to promote their culture. The Americans do little, claiming that their authors are sufficiently popular to require no assistance.

Even when it had books to sell, Tatran experienced troubles with distributors and bookshops. Different groups have been fighting over territory. "Too much depends on contacts, families and even the mafia – they work for themselves, not for publishing." Like Chovanec, Grena is critical of foreign experts coming to Bratislava because a lot of their advice is irrelevant. "Much more useful are attachments to Western publishers where we can select what we need and make contacts".

## Hungarians

A small but important publisher is Kalligram, founded in 1991 to publish the writings of the Hungarian minority in Slovakia in their own language. It quickly became so successful that Hungarian writers from across the border asked it to publish them too. Now it publishes writers from all of Central and Eastern Europe, sometimes in both Slovak and Hungarian, with a separate edition for each book. Its list also includes contemporary American prose, with the emphasis on post-modern.

Starting in 1995, with help from the Open Society Fund, it plans to publish 25 books in Slovak, Hungarian, Polish and Czech, containing representative literature and essays by writers from the eighteenth century to the present. There will be editorial boards in each of the four capitals. George Soros, of course, is seen as enemy number one by Slovak nationalists.

Lajos Grendel, Kalligram's Editor-in-Chief, explains that Kalligram's mission is political as well as literary in so far as it hopes to foster communication between Slovaks and Hungarians, who are often poorly informed about each other by nationalist writers and politicians. Much of the tension between the two communities is manufactured, he believes, and indeed, surveys show that anti-Hungarian feeling is strongest in regions where there are no Hungarians.[25] Among ordinary people, he says, there are no deep conflicts and many mixed marriages. But he fears the situation will deteriorate under the new government. Kalligram has received help from the Pro Slovakia fund and a special fund for minorities. So far, says Grendel cautiously, no strings have been attached.

Distribution is particularly hard. The firm has a one minibus that supplies Slovakia and Hungary, although another distributor handles some of the Slovak books. "If we had more money," says Grendel, "we would invest in a printing house and a better distribution network."

## Journals

Journals have an even harder time than books in Slovakia, and many good ones have folded, particularly in the academic field. Among the precarious survivors is *Fragment*, started by and for underground writers under communism, mainly to translate foreign writers who would not otherwise have been published in Slovakia. Its function above ground remains much the same. It translates and introduces writers from many other countries, including the United States, Switzerland, Poland, Russia and Serbia.

It has only 700 subscribers, of whom 100 are libraries, and it relies heavily on any support it can find. CEEPP has helped it in the past. Now, for each number it must hunt for money. One method is to put out special issues dedicated to particular countries, such as Switzerland and the Netherlands, which then provide support from government or foundations (although the Hungarian government did not support a Hungarian number).

*Fragment* is under increasing strain from the rising prices of film, ink and paper, so it lives on tight margins. It is, however, much respected by those who read it, and clearly fills an important small niche in Slovakia's intellectual life. It could be kept alive with relatively very small injections of assistance. Why does it carry on against such odds? "Because I enjoy it," says Oleg Pastier, the Editor-in-Chief, "and to fill a gap that no one else fills. Who else would translate little-known Russians, Serbs and Poles into Slovak?"

In slightly better shape and with a broader readership is *romboid*, a literary journal edited by Pavel Vilikovsky, a distinguished writer and translator whose brother is Ambassador to London. *romboid* was founded in 1966 by a group around Miroslav Valek, then Minister of Culture. Its literary criticism, poetry, short stories and humour maintain high levels, according to regular readers, and it tries to reach all Slovak writers.

However, its circulation is about 1,000 and falling, with half the number accounted for by subscriptions. It suffers from distribution problems, and many libraries and schools have dropped it. Formerly a monthly, it now appears only 10 times a year. Although its base looks firmer than that of *Fragment*, and it receives some help from Pro Slovakia, its future is uncertain. The new Minister of Culture, Ivan Hudec, used to be a contributor but now seems less friendly, and the new government will be more interested in financing publications that peddle its line. Like *Fragment*, *romboid* can pick up foreign help for single issues devoted to writings from a particular country, such as Norway or Austria.

The survival of critical journals and small independent publishers is particularly important in Slovakia to combat the weight of government-sponsored publications and literature for schools. A group of compliant academics recently produced a textbook on Slovak history, *Dejiny Slovenska*, strongly biased against Hungary and perpetuating the view of Slovakia as eternal victim. A whole generation of 14–18-year-olds is now being exposed to this book, in spite of vigorous criticism from independent intellectuals.

## Conclusions

The overlap of Czech and Slovak publications brings both benefits and problems. On the one hand Slovakia gains a wider choice from its relatively easy access to Czech books and journals. On the other hand the opportunities for Slovak publishers are reduced and external competition is increased.

The blurring of the cultural frontier also makes the Slovak intelligentsia uncertain whether to regard the separation of the two countries as a political mistake to be resisted in cultural and intellectual life, or to accept it and make a conscious effort to develop the Slovak identity by promoting indigenous works and translations, even if such translations duplicate the work of Czech publishers.

Because of the slow pace of reforms, demand for books will be curtailed for years to come by the poverty of the intelligentsia and low education budgets. Modernisation of the infrastructure will be slow, and foreign aid will be regarded with suspicion by both political extremes. Many sources of domestic help for publishing will be tainted by these same forces.

If the definition of Slovak identity is not to be monopolised by nationalists, liberal publications will be heavily dependent on outside help. Many important titles are still unavailable, and there is a huge shortage of basic texts in higher education, especially in sociology, philosophy and new areas of study. Fewer successful publishers than in the Czech Republic are interested in publishing loss-making books for reasons of prestige or intellectual conviction, so more responsibility falls on the smaller houses.

Higher education demands special attention. Capital is urgently needed to modernise libraries, information systems and distribution networks. Some is already arriving through programmes such as the library projects of the Soros and Mellon foundations and Dutch support for mobile libraries, but more is needed. At the same time, quite modest sums would keep alive small liberal publishers and distributors of books and journals whose contribution to the political development of the country is out of proportion to their size.

Given its vulnerable geographical position, unstable politics and halting reforms, Slovakia needs special attention. Independent publishers of books and journals provide one of the few checks on governments that use their power to purvey illiberal ideas through the media and the educational world.

## CONCLUSIONS

It is heart-warming to encounter so much enthusiasm and idealism among the publishers of Central Europe, such dedication to ideas and culture, such determination to survive the harsh winds of the marketplace. Instinctively one wants to help almost every charming, intelligent person one encounters in the small world of quality publishing, every precious book on some obscure poet, every fanciful idea, every new angle on national history, every piece of neglected sociological research and, of course, every request to tap the mainstream of Western culture that still flows somewhat erratically through the area.

After five years of transition, however, one must confront some hard questions. The broad reasons for assisting publishers in Central Europe have been discussed in the introduction to this paper. The issue now is how best to proceed. Is it efficient to continue subsidising individual titles? Are we distorting the market by putting money into books and journals for which there is relatively little demand? Are we, perhaps, providing an artificial life-support system for the activities of small elites with recondite interests who represent an outmoded concept of a Central European intelligentsia? Could the money be better spent on projects that spread their benefits more widely? Anyway, is it not the proper task of Central European countries to nurture their own cultures? Are we guilty of cultural colonialism?

## False issues

Before looking at these questions it may be useful to dispose of two false issues. First, the resentment felt by many Central European publishers at the flood of Western literature that has invaded their countries is understandable but misplaced. The people of Central Europe are as entitled as anyone else to read trash if they want to. Indeed, it is difficult to begrudge them a bit of escapism after so many years of exposure to other types of rubbish. This disappoints their intellectual mentors but it is part of the process of joining the rest of the world. There are worse threats to civilisation than cheap romances and spy thrillers, and for some publishers these earn money that is spent on loss-making quality books. What matters is that good books and journals should *also* be available. This is where the problem lies, and it is a real problem.

Secondly, those in Central Europe who argue that the market should be allowed freer rein, and that subsidies distort it, do not always appreciate how much publishing in the West depends on subsidies of various sorts. There is no such thing as a pure market in the serious book trade. A large part of it depends on publicly funded schools, universities, libraries and research grants, as well as on think tanks, private philanthropy and cross-subsidies within large enterprises. Academic publishing relies heavily on academic authors being paid by their universities or institutions and on libraries then buying their books at high prices. Nearly all serious journals rely on subsidies of some kind except a handful of American publications that reach a worldwide English-speaking readership.

It is, therefore, misguided to argue that the once pampered intellectuals of Central Europe should now face up to the realities of the marketplace. Book markets everywhere in the developed world enjoy some cushioning against that type of "reality". The question for Central Europe is not whether to support publishing but how.

## Achievements

There can be no doubt that the outside support given so far has been very valuable. It has enabled small, dedicated publishers to survive the turmoil of transition, thereby nurturing wider areas of culture. It has brought many important books to the market, sustained seminal journals and built up personal links with the West that have been rewarding for both sides. Doubtless there have been wrong decisions, and doubtless some worthy recipients have been neglected, but a certain amount of improvisation was inevitable.

Indeed, improvisation by small, nimble outfits has mostly been more effective than the efforts of larger, slower and more impersonal organisations. For, while the needs of the area have been studied in depth and detail,[26] few if any of the larger projects envisaged have made much progress so far. The job of assisting publishing through the transition has fallen to a proliferation of smaller initiatives by individuals, foundations and Western governments.

## The problem

The underlying cause of most of the troubles besetting quality publishers in Central Europe is simply the poverty of struggling economies that cannot put enough money into private pockets or government budgets to sustain the quality book trade. Governments are besieged by other demands on their funds and under constant pressure from international lending agencies to cut budget deficits. Tax collection is inefficient and corruption rampant.

As a result, schools, universities, libraries, teachers, students and the intelligentsia as a whole cannot afford to buy enough books to create a healthy market. Prices are then kept down for fear of reducing demand even more, making margins too small to support a proper distribution system, thereby further reducing sales by creating a situation in which even people who want to buy serious books cannot always find them, especially outside capital cities. Nor is there much domestic philanthropy to fund think tanks, research projects or individual books. A hopeful start is being made in the Czech Republic, where a Cultural Fund of Entrepreneurs has been set up in spite of the delay in providing tax relief, but it may be a while before the tycoons of today become the Carnegies and Rockefellers of tomorrow.

A secondary but important factor has been the disorganisation of the transition to a market economy. Inexperienced and insecure governments have been unable to put long-term policies in place or to make the best use of foreign assistance. Parts of the book trade itself have been unprofessional and slow to organise, not surprisingly in view of the new environment in which they have found themselves and the lack of the basic skills required to cope with it. Western aid-providers, while often themselves inept and uncoordinated, have been further confused by the difficulty of finding reliable partners with whom to negotiate, whether in governments or in the book trade.

Thus there are two tasks to be undertaken simultaneously: providing temporary support to sustain quality publishers through the transition, and shaping an environment in which they can flourish over the longer term. Western aid-providers must contribute to both tasks in partnership with publishers and governments of the region,

## Funding single titles

The time has not yet come to stop all funding of individual titles. The transition is not yet over, and there are still many important books and struggling journals that ought to be available even if demand for them is small. Demand is not the only measure of value. But application fatigue is setting in. Publishers find they are spending too much time in search of funds and receiving too little in proportion to the effort they put in. New applicants find it difficult to break into established relationships, and those whose applications are turned down are resentful. Whatever criteria are applied by donors will seem wrong to someone.

## Stimulating demand

It is therefore time to make a gradual transition to more efficient ways of helping more people, primarily by stimulating demand. Only if more books are bought at more realistic prices by more individuals and institutions can a healthy market develop. Ultimately, only economic growth can solve this problem. In the meantime a number of ideas are in circulation.

In the retail market it has been suggested that donors could pay booksellers a percentage of the price of each book sold from an approved list. This would ensure that aid went to books for which there was real demand and would increase booksellers' incentives to stock serious books.

Such a system would, however, be more complicated to administer than direct grants to publishers, and there would be more scope for cheating by slippery bookkeeping. Many publishers are not keen on the idea because they would have to carry the full costs if the book did not sell. Most of them have too little capital to take the risk. There would also be controversy over which books should be on the list. Moreover, the system would not solve the problem of financing books that ought to be available even if demand is low. It is, however, worth further investigation.

A more promising idea is that students should receive grants for buying books. The grants could be in the form of vouchers or, to make cheating more difficult, credit accounts at university bookshops for purchases from an approved list wide enough to provide real choice. A scheme already exists in some Budapest university departments under which students with "smart cards" can purchase books up to a certain limit in university bookshops. If the idea spreads, it will be important to ensure that responsibility for drawing up the list is in suitable hands. Independent arts councils could be an answer, with a committee of academic advisers for the university sector. Selecting books for students would be easier than for the general public but would also be vulnerable to political pressures. Meanwhile, Mr Fiser's bookshop in Kaprova, one of the best in the Czech Republic, has set an example by introducing discounts for students.

Guaranteed purchases are another way of increasing demand. In Norway, the Norwegian Cultural Council buys 1,000 copies of every adult book (children's books are also assisted) and distributes them free to libraries. If a special committee then decides that the quality is too low, the publisher must refund the cost. The idea is to provide support without pre-publication control. The system would be expensive and difficult to transfer to Central Europe but it is an example of a method of assisting publishers and libraries without directly determining what they publish.

## The role of governments

The main responsibility for providing a favourable environment for the book trade falls on the countries of the area themselves. As Jean Gattegno of the Council of Europe has written,[27] "No state can afford to remain indifferent when classic works of the nation's literature and history are no longer available because they are deemed to be non-profitable; when a population that has been encouraged to respect books (one of the distinctive features of 'old regimes') cannot afford to buy them because prices are too high; when libraries are deteriorating through lack of new acquisitions; or when native writers have to find publishers abroad – just like the dissidents of former days – because no one in their own country will take a risk on a new author."

Yet the new democratic governments, caught up in transitional politics, infected by simplistic views of the free market and inhibited by fears of reasserting political control over culture, have been slow to define their attitudes to books. Funding arrangements are still evolving; copyright laws still provide poor protection for publishers; the importance of non-profit organisations in fostering civil society is insufficiently recognised and their legal status inadequate in most countries - a Czech draft law is still, at the time of writing, being resisted by the Prime Minister.

As they move towards membership of the European Union, the Visegrad governments will come under more pressure to align their copyright laws, their taxes and to some extent their educational systems with those of Western Europe. Meanwhile, they should pursue Andras Torok's "safari park" concept, outlined in the Hungarian section above, attempting to improve the environment for quality publishing by measures such as tax concessions, reduced postage rates, capital for information systems, better copyright laws, improved libraries, legislation to encourage non-profit institutions and easier access to capital. In all these areas, Western encouragement and support can be valuable if offered in the right spirit.

## Government subsidies

Where direct government subsidies for books and journals are still necessary it will be important that these should be administered by bodies independent of political control yet sufficiently accountable to be entrusted with public funds. The balance is never easy to find. Memories of the cultural controls of the communist period make for wary relations between independent publishers and governments, especially in those countries where post-communist parties have returned to power. Cooperation has been made even more difficult by mutual suspicion among publishers themselves, who have been slow to organise effective pressure groups.

The idea of independent "arts councils" is gradually catching on. In the Czech Republic a law to set up such a body has been prepared and should be passed soon. Members will be chosen by parliament, subject to a veto by the Minister of Culture which is expected to be only formal. In Poland there is strong pressure to move in the same direction. Hungary already has its Book Foundation under the auspices of the Ministry of Culture and Education although its life has not been smooth. In this area Western experience and mediation could be useful, possibly backed by offers of matching funds.

## Education

A key sector for governments and foreign aid-providers is education. Large amounts of capital and serious government commitments to reform are necessary if real progress is to be made. The governments of the area acknowledge in principle that investment in education should pay off in future prosperity. They would accept the World Bank's dictum: "Higher education is of paramount importance for economic and social development."[28] But they have difficulty dragging sufficient money out of hard-pressed finance ministries to put the principle into practice. Nor are they always clear about what they want. Education policies have been started, stopped and diverted as governments changed.[29] World Bank projects have been stalled by indecision and inter-departmental friction, while loans for education have been resisted.

The economic case for investing in education can be difficult to sustain when it comes to financing books on obscure poets or ancient history. That requires belief in intellectual trickle-down. In principle, ideas generated in specialised circles, even if of no immediate practical value, should contribute to the enrichment of intellectual life as a whole, the benefits of which are then disseminated through teachers and specialised journals to students, the media and a wider public. How far this actually happens is difficult to measure. It may well be that some of the more obscure areas of scholarship will have to wait until more public funds are available, meanwhile relying on electronic distribution or accessibility in English or German.

It is in the mainstream of education that the needs are greatest, often not in the elite universities of capital cities, although they are struggling too, but in the schools and universities of the provinces where most of the next generation are receiving their education. The need is less for heavy-weight specialist books than for a range of standard works in different fields on which students and teachers can draw.

The ability to evaluate, compare and select from difference sources was positively discouraged under the old system, when one text or set of texts was prescribed for each subject. In a modern educational system these are probably the most important skills of all, and vital to the proper functioning of liberal democracy, Thus the whole nature of education in Central Europe will have to change, putting new demands on educational publishers. A variety of books must be continuously available across the country with publishers competing for the attention of teachers and students and offering choice at all levels. Pointing the way is the programme of the Central European University Press in Budapest for translating about 100 basic classics of political thought into all the local languages of the former Soviet bloc.

On the negative side, the stubborn survival of *scripta* is inhibiting change. These individually produced lecture notes divert scarce resources from books and isolate universities from each other. A few are good but many are not, and quality control is uneven. In no way can they be a proper substitute for books. Unfortunately universities and teachers have a vested interest in them because they bring in money, but recent research in Hungary shows that they also cost a great deal in terms of teachers' time, university facilities and duplicated effort, even within universities.[30]

## Libraries

Libraries must be at the centre of any help for the book trade. University, school and public libraries all lack money to buy the books and journals they need, particularly foreign journals. Some of their budgets have scarcely changed since they were set for the purchase of a limited range of approved books. Many are in outdated premises with poorly-trained staff, patchy catalogues and little or no modern technology. They can neither service their customers effectively nor generate the level of demand that the book trade needs. Administrative confusion often makes matters worse by dividing responsibility for libraries among local authorities and different government bodies.

Western aid has been similarly diffuse. According to Richard Ayres in a very critical report, "most work could be described as piecemeal, depending on bilateral contacts between institutions and personal, rather than institutional, enthusiasm. The challenge is now to develop a multilateral forum for the exchange of information based on self-interest and cooperation rather than 'aid'. Too many training programmes are Western initiatives, not responses to local needs or requests."[31]

The most effective so far, says Ayres, have been those of the Mellon and Soros foundations. Extremely useful, too, is the network of partnerships and bilateral agreements that has grown up among libraries and librarians involving personal exchanges and many forms of modest help. Western librarians often give help in their own time, and Ayres suggests their replacement cover at home might be funded so that they can stay abroad longer. Among the formal partnerships is that involving the British Council, The British Library, the Library Association and International Book Development Ltd to undertake and stimulate research into library and information services.[32]

All these efforts make only a relatively small impact. For broad systemic change, substantial sums of capital are needed. But the difficulties of getting large projects under way are exemplified by the fate of the World Bank project to provide new textbooks and modernised libraries in Hungary. Despite years of preparatory work it has been stalled by a combination of changing priorities and confusion in the Hungarian government, pressure from lobbies that want to preserve state production of textbooks, political opposition to taking on more debt, and disagreements within the World Bank between those who believe the private sector is ready to meet the demand for textbooks and those who think its development should be financed first. Clearly, a multitude of effective smaller projects is preferable to one stalled giant.

## New technology

The information revolution should attract the special attention of foreign donors. It is potentially one of the best allies of democracy and intellectual freedom because it creates a global information marketplace largely beyond government control. It will have a dramatic impact on libraries, higher education and general publishing. In the book market alone, a German expert has predicted that electronic publishing will account for about 20 per cent of the industry's sales by the year 2000, mainly in dictionaries and reference works.[33]

At present it is creeping only slowly into the Visegrad Four, held back by lack of capital and poor telephone lines. CD-ROM provides an interim solution for certain types of information, particularly bibliographies and reference books. When on-line systems become more common in Central Europe, universities should be the first to benefit from instant access to catalogues and journal articles from all over the world. The cost of document transfer will be significant because Central Europe will buy more information than it sells, so this is an area where modest foreign subsidies could have a broad effect.[34]

The idea that Central European libraries might skip a generation by jumping straight to the pure electronic library is tempting but would probably not be feasible.[35] Paper copies will remain more cost-effective for publications in heavy use, leaving lightly used material for electronic delivery. Even so, publishers are concerned that electronic document delivery will be used by libraries to avoid the purchase of journals.[36]

New technology should also improve the economics of book publishing. This will be particularly important in making reprints cheaper. In the past, a publisher would choose a book and publish it. Intellectuals would buy it, discuss it, and sometimes recommend it to a wider public. Then it would be sold out. Now the whole nature of intellectual discourse is changing. Like students, readers need regular access to a range of titles that are reprinted when demand warrants. The economics of publishing must therefore change to accommodate smaller runs, larger stocks and facilities for quick reprints. At the moment, it is extremely difficult to keep a book continuously in print because of poor distribution, expensive storage and fluctuations in paper prices.

The DocuTech machine already marketed by Xerox can scan books, store them electronically and re-print them much more cheaply than conventional presses. As this type of machine becomes cheaper and more widely available the economics of reprints and short runs should change dramatically, making it easier to maintain a constant supply of books for which demand is low but regular. With outside help, the machines could be bought either by large publishers or, preferably, by independent enterprises that rent out time to all comers, perhaps giving preferential or assisted rates to small quality publishers. Production quality would, however, suffer.

Only slightly further ahead lies the possibility of transmitting whole books electronically and then printing them out cheaply at the other end. University libraries will then not need such large stocks because they will be able to call up books on demand. But copyright problems will become even more acute than they are already with electronically transmitted journals.

University teaching may also be revolutionised by the spread of fibre-optic networks, such as SuperJanet in Britain. Lecturers will be able to address almost any number of audiences simultaneously and take questions from them. University College London has already tried transmitting surgery lectures to six universities at once, with graphics, X-ray slides and video sequences of operations, followed by questions. When developed, this will mean that students can learn from the best specialists wherever they are.[37] The implications for the general run of teaching below that level, however may be less comfortable.

Capital and entrepreneurial spirit will be needed to make the best use of new technology. Small injections of capital for equipment and training can have far-reaching effects and are often easier to arrange than large projects.

## Distribution

Capital and new technology are also needed to improve distribution systems, which are a particularly promising area for Western help. The most pressing needs are computerised information and invoicing, training in advertising and promotion and above all more cooperation among publishers, who in several countries have found it difficult to understand that competition does not preclude cooperation in areas of common interest. Outside encouragement and mediation could be helpful here.

The Netherlands has probably the best distribution system in Europe, and its expertise has been made available. Its Centraal Boekhuis in Culemborg, founded by publishers and booksellers, offers a model for small countries. It is probably too large and expensive to be copied, even if Central Europe's publishers could be persuaded to cooperate, since it distributes more than 36 million books a year, but scaled-down versions might be set up with international help.

## Rights

All the countries in the area fall short of providing a satisfactory legislative framework for trade in rights and licenses. In varying degrees, all have yet to free themselves fully from the period in which intellectual property was viewed as belonging entirely to the author and/or the state, rather than the publisher. The concept of rights, including subsidiary rights, as tradeable items in a burgeoning information industry is still sparsely understood, so Central Europe could become isolated from the rest of developed world on this issue. Meanwhile, because of the lag, publishers lack the means and incentives to get behind their books as fully as they would do in the West. Western support for copyright reform is therefore still needed.

## Journals

Special attention should be given to independent journals, none of which could survive without financial support. Critics dismiss them as playpens for intellectuals but they have always played an important role in Central Europe and still do so, even in changing conditions. Indeed, their role could even increase in places where post-communist governments and foreign conglomerates are acquiring disproportionate power in the media. They provide a forum for independent thinking and debate, a point of contact with foreign writers and, through their reviews, stimulus for the book trade and the arts in general. As in the West, they can initiate and develop themes that are then taken up in the more popular media. Without them, conformist thinking would have an easier ride. Only small sums are needed to keep the best of them alive. It is money well spent.

## Capital

A theme running through the laments of almost all Central European publishers and distributors is the difficulty of raising capital. For some enterprises the problem is lack of collateral but for most it is the crippling cost of borrowing at high interest rates. There are some low-interest credits available through international agencies but they seldom seem to come the way of publishers or distributors of books. If foreign aid-providers could find ways of making low-interest loans available on flexible conditions to the book trade without distorting the competitive environment (a difficult task) they could greatly improve the outlook for small publishers and distributors.

## Literary Agents

Many Central European publishers complain about the literary agents through whom they have to deal with American and other Western publishers. They are particularly aggrieved about the agencies of Gerd

Plessl and his former colleagues, which they regard as unnecessary, expensive and often inefficient. Their pride is involved as they would like to feel important and "normal" enough to engage in direct negotiation. In this they often overestimate themselves, failing to see how small they are in relation to Western publishing conglomerates. Agents are a time-saving convenience for distant Americans with little knowledge of Central Europe and no time to find out whether they are dealing with a large, established publisher or some near-bankrupt amateur operating out of a back room.[38]

Yet it is not difficult to sympathise with the Central Europeans, too, who feel that the Iron Curtain still exists in many Western minds. The Polish Chamber of Books is setting up its own rights centre, and there is talk of similar action in other countries. Western help could be useful in encouraging direct negotiations where possible, particularly with American publishers. The problem is, however, confined mainly to trade publishers, since academic and educational publishers in Europe and the United States have long dealt directly with the region and have no need of agents.

## Training

Several publishers interviewed for this study said Western training schemes in their own countries had lost their value. Some were critical of these schemes, particularly those run by the Americans, Germans and French. They prefer attachment programmes that bring them into close contact with Western publishers, such as those run from Britain by IBD, the Publishers Association and, until recently, CEEPP.[39]

There is, however, a case for shifting the emphasis of training to middle management in the publishing industry, where the lack of basic skills is still a serious handicap, making delegation difficult and inhibiting growth. Local training at this level could be combined with attachments in the West for senior and middle management.[40]

## Local philanthropy

It is important during this formative stage in the development of a business culture to encourage the creation of a philanthropic tradition. Western help can be useful not only in drafting the relevant laws but also in providing, for instance, advice from Western philanthropists to Central European business associations on why and how to engage in philanthropy, and in promoting ideas such as the award of honorary titles to philanthropists from associations of writers and translators.

## Information on sources of funding

One of the obstacles to more effective help is the lack of information on the multiplicity of programmes that are either in operation or on offer from foreign aid-providers. This has confused applicants and caused programmes to overlap and compete, thereby wasting resources. There should be an information centre – on no account with power – where all programmes are registered and regularly updated, and where applicants can make their needs known if they wish. Pubwatch in New York with CEEPP in Oxford has assembled a valuable directory of Western organisations that assist book culture in Central and Eastern Europe, but a larger data base continuously updated on projects in progress would help donors as well as applicants and reduce duplication of effort. Pubwatch tried this and was discouraged by widespread reluctance to provide information. Efforts should, however, continue. At the same time Western organisations could expand their valuable work of assembling and distributing information on all aspects of the Central European book market.

## Cultural interchange, not exports only

A criticism often made of foreign governments and foundations is that they promote their own national or sectoral interests and are not sufficiently flexible in their views of Europe's cultural needs. Britain, for instance, promotes low-priced business books in English, which are then denied translation rights in any country in the area – an absurdly restrictive policy. It also foolishly provides no money for translating English books into local languages. The Americans, French, Germans, Swiss, Austrians and others think it worthwhile supporting translations into Central European languages, although they are sometimes criticised for taking a too restricted view of the type of book that should be helped. The European Union's PHARE programme is also widely condemned for being slow and bureaucratic.

A symptom of narrow thinking is that the main emphasis on Western assistance has been on fostering the export of Western books and ideas to Central Europe instead of promoting broad networks of cultural interchange. This is to some extent inevitable while overcoming years of isolation, and the tendency will persist because of the disproportionate weight of the English-speaking world. It is also inevitable that governments answering to taxpayers will emphasise promotion of national interests.

But cultural trade would be healthier if more help were given to interchange among the Visegrad Four and the export of writings from Central Europe to the West, both fiction and non-fiction. The Soros Foundation has a valuable "East–East" programme for journals and newspapers. CEEPP has done something to remedy the neglect of classic Central European fiction by launching a series of Central European classics translated into English. This will continue with the support of a CEEPP successor organisation, the Central European Classics Trust. The Czech government is putting in place a fund to promote outward translations of Czech writings. But more could be done to promote a healthier cultural trade balance. The West needs to learn as well as teach.

## Professional contacts

One of the areas in which flexible, informal help can be valuable is in fostering the growth of professional contacts in the publishing world and among libraries. A great deal is already happening here that is not always visible. There are links among publishers associations, joint ventures between individual publishing houses, exchanges among libraries, and cooperative arrangements among journals, such as that between *Buksz* of Budapest and the *Times Literary Supplement* and the *New York Review of Books*. Precisely where foreign assistance can be most usefully injected is not always easy to identify but it is important to remain alert and supportive towards these areas of productive professional activity.

## Last thoughts

The worst of the pains of transition are probably over. Publishers are learning professional skills; public funding for books is evolving; governments are slowly providing better legal protection; and more money is gradually reaching the pockets of consumers, allowing book prices to rise. Even the smaller language areas are coming to see that they need not be swamped by foreign interests or allow their cultures to be destroyed. Like the Netherlands and Scandinavian countries, they can have flourishing indigenous publishing industries if they create the right environment.

Nevertheless, in all the Visegrad countries a great deal more remains to be done before an adequate range of quality books is available for the general public and the educational sectors. The market is still underdeveloped, and liberal democracy is not yet so well established that the emergence of a healthy and diverse publishing sector can be taken for granted.

Although the main responsibility for fostering a lively book trade must rest with the countries themselves, foreign assistance will remain extremely important for years to come if these struggling democracies are to reconnect fully with the rest of Europe.

## NOTES

1 Resolution of the Working Group on Art and Culture of the SPD Parliamentary Group on the occasion of the 1993 Frankfurt Book Fair.

2 Among many writings on the subject of reconnecting with history see "Political Uses of Tradition in Postcommunist East Central Europe", *Social Research*, New York, Volume 60, No. 4, Winter 1993.

3 Igor Hajek, "Czech Culture in the Cauldron", *Europe–Asia Studies*, Vol. 46, No. 1, 1994, pp. 127–142.

4 *Polish Libraries Today*, National Library, Warsaw, Volume 2, 1993.

5 Norman Davies, *God's Playground* (Oxford University Press, 1981), Volume II, p. 233.

6 *Notes Wydawniczy*, quoted in *European Bookseller*, May/June 1994.

7 Paper presented by Andrzej Rosner at a conference co-sponsored by Pubwatch, New York, and the Council of Europe in Strasbourg in 1993

8 ibid.

9 ibid.

10 For these comments on rights I am indebted to Lynette Owen, Rights and Contracts Director of Longman Group UK.

11 John F. Baker, "Publishing in Central Europe", *The Publishers Weekly*, 5 September 1994.

12 John F. Baker, op. cit.

13 *Nepszabadsag*, Budapest, 3 December 1994.

14 Igor Hajek, op. cit.

15 Ivan Klima "An Upheaval for Czech Readers", *New York Review of Books*, 20 October 1994.

16 ibid.

17 ibid.

18 *European Bookseller*, October 1994.

19 Ivan Klima, op.cit.

20 For a lengthy discussion of Slovakia's view of itself, as reflected in its literature, see Robert B. Pynsent, *Killing, Laughing and Observing, Three Trends in Contemporary Slovak Literature*, School of Slavonic and East European Studies, University of London, forthcoming.

21 *Current Problems of Slovakia*, May 1994, Center for Social and Market Analysis, Bratislava.

22 Maria Hrabinska, "The Process of Diversification of Postsecondary Education in Slovakia", *European Journal of Education*, Vol. 29, No. 1, 1994.

23 *Chronicle of Higher Education*, 13 April 1994.

24 See also Eduard Sarmir and Stefan Zajac, *Higher Education and Research in the Slovak Republic: Major changes since 1989*, Institute for Human Sciences, Vienna, December 1993.

25 Martin Butora and Zora Butorova, "Slovakia: The identity challenges of the newly born state", *Social Research*, New York, Winter 1993.

26 Notably by International Book Development of London.

27 *European Bookseller*, May/June 1994.

28 *Higher Education, The Lessons from Experience*, World Bank, Washington DC, May 1994.

29 For an expert overview of higher education and research in all four countries see *Transformation of the National Higher Education and Research Systems of Central Europe, Volume 7, Issues in Transition*, Institute for Human Sciences, Vienna, October 1994.

30 Report by International Book Development Ltd, London, for the Hungarian Ministry of Culture and Education, January 1995.

31 Richard Ayres, *Review of Member State Actions in Central and Eastern Europe*, on behalf of the European Commission for the Council of Europe workshop on library development, Strasbourg, 3–4 February 1994.

32 Runnals Davis, International Officer, The Library Association, 7 Ridgmount Street, London WC1E 7AE, paper on "The Library Association and the New Europe: Library Achievements and Opportunities in Professional Cooperation, 1994".

33 Eugen Emmerling, Chairman of the Federation of German Book Publishers, in a radio interview at the 1994 Frankfurt Book Fair.

34 Graham P. Cornish, *International Library Cooperation: Uniting or Dividing Europe?* International Federation of Library Associations and Institutions, British Library Document Supply Centre, Boston Spa, Wetherby, West Yorkshire, LS23 7BQ,

35 Richard Ayres, op. cit.

36 F.J. Friend, Librarian, University College London, Gower Street, London WC1E 6BT, paper delivered at the Prague Book Fair, May 1994.

37 *The Independent*, London, 12 December 1995.

38 For both sides see John F. Baker, op.cit.

39 A Senior Managers' Attachment Programme was set up in London in 1992 under the auspices of the Publishers Association's East Europe Working Party and CEEPP, funded by the Conanima Foundation in Switzerland and the Know-How Fund of the British Foreign Office.

40 *Book Industry Training for East Central Europe and the Former Soviet Union, University Link Training Scheme*, project proposal by International Book Development, London, February 1995.

# *100 BOOKS*
## *which have influenced Western public discourse since the Second World War*

For the origins of the list that appears overleaf, see above, p. 41. An initial list was put together by a small panel consisting of Robert Cassen, Ralf Dahrendorf, Timothy Garton Ash, Michael Ignatieff, Leszek Kolakowski and Bryan Magee. It was then revised following an extensive discussion at the last meeting of CEEPP Trustees. With very few exceptions, authors are represented by only one title. Works of fiction are included only when they had a wider impact on public discourse. Books by trustees are not included.

Titles are grouped in decades by the date of their first appearance. In all cases the English title is mentioned first and the original title in [ ]. Within decades the order is alphabetical.

To begin with, there are certain seminal works which were published *before the Second World War* but which had a major influence on post-war discourse. The list would certainly include:

Karl Barth: *Credo*

Marc Bloch: *Feudal Society* [La Société féodale]

Martin Buber: *I and Thou* [Ich und Du]

Nobert Elias: *The Civilizing Process* [Über den Prozess der Zivilisation]

Sigmund Freud: *Civilization and its Discontents* [Das Unbehagen in der Kultur]

Élie Halévy:*The Era of Tyrannies. Essays on socialism and war* [L'Ère des tyrannies. Études sur le socialisme et la guerre]

Martin Heidegger: *Being and Time* [Sein und Zeit]

Johan Huizinga: *The Waning of the Middle Ages* [Herfsttij der Middeleeuwen]

Aldous Huxley: *Brave New World*

Franz Kafka: *The Castle* [Das Schloss]

John Maynard Keynes: *The Economic Consequences of the Peace*

John Maynard Keynes: *The General Theory of Employment, Interest and Money*

Lewis Namier: *The Structure of Politics at the Accession of George III*

Jose Ortega y Gasset: *The Revolt of the Masses* [La Rebelion de las masas]

Karl Popper: *The Logic of Scientific Discovery* [Logik der Forschung]

Bertrand Russell: (A new selection of his essays)

Ludwig Wittgenstein: *Tractatus logico-philosophicus* [Logisch-Philosophische Abhandlung]

## Books of the 1940s

1. Simone de Beauvoir: *The Second Sex* [Le Deuxième Sexe]
2. Marc Bloch: *The Historian's Craft* [Apologie pour l'histoire, ou, Métier d'historien]
3. Fernand Braudel: *The Mediterranean and the Mediterranean World in the Age of Philip II* [La Méditerranée et le monde méditerranéen à l'époque de Philippe II]
4. James Burnham: *The Managerial Revolution*
5. Albert Camus: *The Myth of Sisyphus* [Le Mythe de Sisyphe]
6. Albert Camus: *The Outsider* [L'Étranger]
7. R.G. Collingwood: *The Idea of History*
8. Erich Fromm: *The Fear of Freedom* [Die Furcht vor der Freiheit]
9. Max Horkheimer and Theodor W Adorno: *Dialectic of Enlightenment* [Dialektik der Aufklärung]
10. Karl Jaspers: *The Perennial Scope of Philosophy* [Der philosophische Glaube]
11. Arthur Koestler: *Darkness at Noon*
12. André Malraux: *Man's Fate* [La Condition humaine]
13. Franz Neumann: *Behemoth: The Structure and Practice of National Socialism*
14. George Orwell: *Animal Farm*
15. George Orwell: *Nineteen Eighty-four*
16. Karl Polanyi: *The Great Transformation*
17. Karl Popper: *The Open Society and its Enemies*
18. Paul Samuelson: *Economics. An Introductory Analysis*
19. Jean-Paul Sartre: *Existentialism and Humanism* [L'Existentialisme est un humanisme]
20. Joseph Schumpeter: *Capitalism, Socialism and Democracy*
21. Martin Wight: *Power Politics*

## Books of the 1950s

22. Hannah Arendt: *The Origins of Totalitarianism*
23. Raymond Aron: *The Opium of the Intellectuals* [L'Opium des intellectuels]
24. Kenneth Arrow: *Social Choice and Individual Values*
25. Roland Barthes: *Mythologies*
26. Winston Churchill: *The Second World War*
27. Norman Cohn: *The Pursuit of the Millennium*
28. Milovan Djilas: *The New Class. An analysis of the Communist system*
29. Mircea Eliade: *Images and Symbols* [Images et symboles]
30. Erik Erikson: *Young Man Luther. A study in psychoanalysis and history*
31. Lucien Febvre: *The Struggle for History* [Combat pour l'histoire]
32. John Kenneth Galbraith: *The Affluent Society*
33. Erving Goffman: *The Presentation of Self in Everyday Life*
34. Arthur Koestler and Richard Crossman (eds): *The God that Failed. Six studies in Communism*
35. Primo Levi: *If this is a Man* [Se questo è un uomo]
36. Claude Levi-Strauss: *A World on the Wane* [Tristes tropiques]
37. Czeslaw Milosz: *The Captive Mind* [Zniewolony umysl]
38. Boris Pasternak: *Doctor Zhivago*
39. David Riesman: *The Lonely Crowd*
40. Herbert Simon: *Models of Man, Social and Rational*
41. C.P. Snow: *The Two Cultures and the Scientific Revolution*
42. Leo Strauss: *Natural Right and History*
43. J.L. Talmon: *The Origins of Totalitarian Democracy*
44. A.J.P. Taylor: *The Struggle for Mastery in Europe*
45. Arnold Toynbee: *A Study of History*

46. Karl Wittfogel: *Oriental Despotism. A comparative study of total power*
47. Ludwig Wittgenstein: *Philosophical Investigations* [Philosophische Untersuchungen]

## Books of the 1960s

48. Hannah Arendt: *Eichmann in Jerusalem. A report on the banality of evil*
49. Daniel Bell: *The End of Ideology*
50. Isaiah Berlin: *Four Essays on Liberty*
51. Albert Camus: *Notebooks 1935–1951* [Carnets]
52. Elias Canetti: *Crowds and Power* [Masse und Macht]
53. Robert Dahl: *Who Governs? Democracy and Power in an American City*
54. Mary Douglas: *Purity and Danger*
55. Erik Erikson: *Gandhi's Truth. On the origins of militant nonviolence*
56. Michael Foucault: *Madness and civilization: a history of insanity in the Age of Reason* [Histoire de la folie à l'âge classique]
57. Milton Friedman: *Capitalism and Freedom*
58. Alexander Gerschenkron: *Economic Backwardness in Historical Perspective*
59. Antoni Gramsci: *Prison Notebooks* [Quaderni del carcere]
60. Herbert Hart: *The Concept of Law*
61. Friedrich von Hayek: *The Constitution of Liberty* [Die Verfassung der Freiheit]
62. Jane Jacobs: *The Death and Life of Great American Cities*
63. Carl Gustav Jung: *Memories, Dreams, Reflections* [Erinnerungen, Träume, Gedanken]
64. Thomas Kuhn: *The Structure of Scientific Revolutions*

65. Emmanuel Le Roy Ladurie: *The Peasants of Languedoc* [Les Paysans de Languedoc]
66. Claude Lévi-Strauss: *The Savage Mind* [La Pensée sauvage]
67. Konrad Lorenz: *On Aggression* [Das sogenannte Böse]
68. Thomas Schelling: *The Strategy of Conflict*
69. Fritz Stern: *The Politics of Cultural Despair*
70. E.P. Thompson: *The Making of the English Working Class*

## Books of the 1970s

71. Daniel Bell: *The Cultural Contradictions of Capitalism*
72. Isaiah Berlin: *Russian Thinkers*
73. Ronald Dworkin: *Taking Rights Seriously*
74. Clifford Geertz: *The Interpretation of Cultures*
75. Albert Hirschman: *Exit, voice, and loyalty*
76. Leszek Kolakowski: *Main Currents of Marxism* [Glowne nurty marksizmu]
77. Hans Küng: *On Being a Christian* [Christ Sein]
78. Robert Nozick: *Anarchy, State and Utopia*
79. John Rawls: *A Theory of Justice*
80. Gershom Scholem: *The Messianic Idea in Judaism, and other essays on Jewish spirituality*
81. Ernst Friedrich Schumacher: *Small is Beautiful*
82. Tibor Scitovsky: *The Joyless Economy*
83. Quentin Skinner: *The Foundations of Modern Political Thought*
84. Alexander Solzhenitsyn: *The Gulag Archipelago*
85. Keith Thomas: *Religion and the Decline of Magic*

## Books of the 1980s and beyond:

86. Raymond Aron: *Memoirs* [Mémoires]
87. Peter Berger: *The Capitalist Revolution: fifty propositions about prosperity, equality and liberty*
88. Norberto Bobbio: *The Future of Democracy* [Il futuro della democrazia, 1985]
89. Karl Dietrich Bracher: *The Totalitarian Experience* [Die totalitare Erfahrung]
90. John Eatwell, Murray Milgate and Peter Newman (eds): *The New Palgrave: the world of economics*
91. Ernest Gellner: *Nations and nationalism*
92. Vaclav Havel: *Living in Truth*
93. Stephen Hawking: *A Brief History of Time*
94. Paul Kennedy: *The Rise and Fall of the Great Powers*
95. Milan Kundera: *The Book of Laughter and Forgetting*
96. Primo Levi: *The Drowned and the Saved* [I sommersi e i salvati]
97. Roger Penrose: *The Emperor's New Mind: concerning computers, minds, and the laws of physics*
98. Richard Rorty: *Philosophy and the mirror of nature*
99. Amartya Sen: *Resources, values and development*
100. Michael Walzer: *Spheres of Justice*